SAXOPHONE FOR BEGINNERS

Comprehensive Beginner's Guide To Learn The Art Of Playing Saxophone From A-Z

RHYTHM DIVINE STUDIO

© Copyright 2021 - **All rights reserved.**

You are hereby instructed not to reproduce, duplicate, or use the contents of this book without direct written permission from the author.

The publisher is not responsible for your use of this book so you may not in any circumstance blame or hold him or her to legal responsibility for any reparation, compensations, or monetary forfeiture owing to the information included herein in any direct or indirect way.

Legal Notice:

This book has copyright protection. You can use the book for personal purposes. You should not sell, alter, use, alter, quote, distribute, or paraphrase in part or whole the material contained in this book without obtaining the permission of the author first.

Disclaimer Notice:

You must also bear in mind that the information in this document is for entertainment and casual reading purposes only. We attempt to give accurate, up to date and reliable information. You do not get warranties of any kind. The persons who read admit that the writer is not giving legal, financial, medical, or other advice. We sourced this book's content from various places. You must consult a licensed professional in this field if you want to try any techniques shown in this book.

By going through this document, the booklover comes to an agreement that under no situation is the author accountable for any forfeiture, direct or indirect, which they may incur because of the use of any material from this document, including, but not limited to, — errors, omissions, or inaccuracies.

CONTENTS

INTRODUCTION		1
CHAPTER 1	Play The Saxophone - A Saxophonist	3
CHAPTER 2	The Four Saxes	16
CHAPTER 3	Buying A Saxophone	25
CHAPTER 4	The Body	33
CHAPTER 5	Parts Of The Saxophone	39
CHAPTER 6	The Saxophone Mouthpiece	48
CHAPTER 7	Saxophones For Beginners	53
CHAPTER 8	Major Scales On The Saxophone	72
CHAPTER 9	Beginner Soprano Saxophone Techniques	90
CHAPTER 10	Saxophone Articulation	102
CHAPTER 11	Musical Modes Explained	105
CHAPTER 12	Create Practice Methods And Stay Inspired	118
CHAPTER 13	Saxophone Maintenance Tips	124
CHAPTER 14	Myths About The Saxophone	130
CONCLUSION		140
REFERENCES		141

INTRODUCTION

Music truly is the most beautiful thing in the world, whether you have artistic desires or want a new hobby, whether you want to listen or to play. If it's learning a new instrument, there is no better instrument than the saxophone.

The saxophone is a loud, dominant instrument and an integral part of the marching bands. If you want to express yourself boldly, learn to play the saxophone. In this book, "Saxophone for Beginners," you will learn everything you need to know about this wonderful instrument.

You will cover the theory of music, right up to how to approach playing the sax. Invented by Adolphe Sax, it is a relatively new instrument, and you won't find music written for it by the old masters like Mozart, Chopin, or Beethoven. Over time, many adaptations have been made and now we have many pieces that give the horn its share of the spotlight.

You will also learn the different components of the saxophone and how to assemble it and keep it clean. We'll also provide you with an in-depth look at some of the best saxophones for beginners and intermediate players and delve into whether you should rent or buy when you are just starting out.

Learning to play a new instrument is not easy and it requires a whole heap of practice and patience. When it all finally comes together, you will realize that the hard work was well worth the effort.

CHAPTER 1

PLAY THE SAXOPHONE - A SAXOPHONIST

Professional saxophonists produce clear, perfect notes easily and many people don't realize how much blood, sweat, and tears have gone into getting that far, the saxophone is one of the most versatile instruments and finds a place in many different music styles, orchestras and bands.

VARIOUS COLLEGE AND SCHOOL BANDS

The saxophone allows you to transit from jazz to classical music, from rock to Latin and soul. This is because you can influence the sound of the instrument to a large extent. The saxophone is equally at home with all these styles. It is natural for the saxophone to be a part of the college and high school bands, marching bands that perform in parades and on stage or in the middle of football games and these bands go by many names - jazz bands, concert bands, and wind bands, each with sixty to a hundred members.

Funk, Rock, or Jazz Band

You can join the rock sections of the rock, funk, or jazz band and add spunky riffs or melodious harmonies to the music. Saxophone solos are rare in such music, but they are the key feature in jazz ensembles. Popular formats are the jazz quartet, with the saxophone, drums, piano, and double bass or quintet, and sometimes including a second saxophonist or trumpet player.

The Saxophone is Young

It is not usual to find the saxophone in the standard lineup of a symphony orchestra because Beethoven, Mozart, and other classical composers died before Adolphe Sax invented his instrument in 1840. Lots of compositions have undergone adaptation for the sax and later composers have produced music for the saxophone. Names of some well-known composers are Maurice Ravel, Hector Berlioz, Richard Strauss, and Bela Bartok.

There are many formats for the sax player apart from the orchestras and bands. For instance, there are compositions for saxophone solos duets for the saxophone and piano, or two saxophones and, in older music, there are duets for flute and oboe too. There is even music written for the saxophone quartet. This music ranges from improvised music to jazz children's songs and hymns. A similar range of works is available for a larger type of ensemble, the saxophone choir.

It's Like Singing

We compare saxophone playing to singing, referring to both the ease and the fluency with which we do both. It is as expressive as your voice and it is as easy to play the saxophone out of tune as it is to sing out of tune. So, while playing the saxophone, make sure you are playing it in tune.

ALTO OR TENOR SAXOPHONES

The saxophones come in various sizes and the most widely used are the alto saxophone and the lower-sounding tenor sax. Their sound suits different varieties of music and they are easier to master than other types. Most players start on one of these horns.

SOPRANO AND BARITONE

The next two saxophones are small, the high-pitched soprano and big, low-toned baritone. Saxophone players usually specialize in one of the four voices and play all four of them. But there are more than the four we normally see. Though they look different, they are the same in their build with the same arrangement of keys. They only vary in size.

HORNS AND SAXOPHONES

Since saxophone is a large word, the players usually refer to them as the sax and the musicians as saxists. Most players call their instrument the horn, which is the common term used by the trumpeters and other brass players.

CURVED SOPRANO, ALTO, AND TENOR SAXOPHONES

When you see all the keys and rods, it will seem that the sax is a complicated instrument. But in reality, it is not.

THE TUBE WITH HOLES

The sax is a long tube with holes. To play the lowest note, close all the holes. The tone goes up one pitch level when you open the last hole nearest the bell. The bell is the flared part of the instrument while the mouthpiece is at the other end. Again, open one hole, and the pitch rises.

The Keys

You will find the tone holes are far apart and the holes too big to cover with your fingertips. Also, there are more tone holes than you have fingers, so we use keys to close the tone holes.

Body, Neck, and Bell

The sax body is the large part covered with keys and holes and it has the neck on the top. The wide flaring part is the bell.

The Mouthpiece and Reed

On the top part of the neck, the mouthpiece and reed remain attached. The reed is a thin piece of cane that generates the sound, and it is held in place by a ligature.

Sound

When we sing or talk, our vocal cords vibrate, caused by the air vibrating around the cords. In the saxophone, you make the reed vibrate, and when it does, the air column in the sax vibrates.

Low Notes from Long Tube

When we close all the holes of the sax and blow it, we get the lowest note. To play higher notes, we open one or more holes. When you open all the holes, you get the highest note.

Pads

The holes must remain closed properly (with no air escaping) to get the proper note. The key cups that cover the holes have pads fitted on them. These felt discs remain covered with soft leather and help seal the tone holes.

Resonators

We have a small metal or plastic disc in the middle of each pad. This is the resonator that helps make the sound of the instrument bright.

Flaring Out

The body of the sax becomes wider as we approach the bell. As the saxophone gets wider, the tone holes get bigger. The one on the neck is the smallest, called the neck octave vent, while the largest tone hole is at the opposite end of the bell. It is also right to assume that the bell itself is the biggest tone hole as it makes the lowest note.

Nine Digits and Twenty-Five Keys

Using eight fingers and one thumb, you can operate all the holes with the key system.

Springs

When you are not playing the instrument, about half the keys of the sax remain open. There is a needle spring in each key that closes the key shut after you opened it.

Felts and Corks

Small bumpers made of cork and felt stop the metal parts from making too much noise. They help some keys close and open simultaneously and determine how far open the key must remain.

Key Guard

These key guards help protect some of the most vulnerable key cups from damage.

Thumb Hook and Thumb Rest

Place the right thumb under the thumb hook to support the instrument. The left thumb goes on the thumb rest and operates the octave key.

Hanger Loop

Saxophones need the support of the sling or the neck strap. The hanger loop for the strap hook is halfway up the back of the body.

The Keys

Sax players use different names for the keys of their instrument. What one player calls a pearl key, another calls the finger pad. These are the primary names of the keys:

The System

The full system of springs, keys, rods, and related moving parts is called the key system, key work, action, or mechanism.

Keys and Key Cups

You press the key to open and close the tone hole. The pad cups or key cups stop the tone holes. Most saxophonists use the terms key for everything, including keys and key cups.

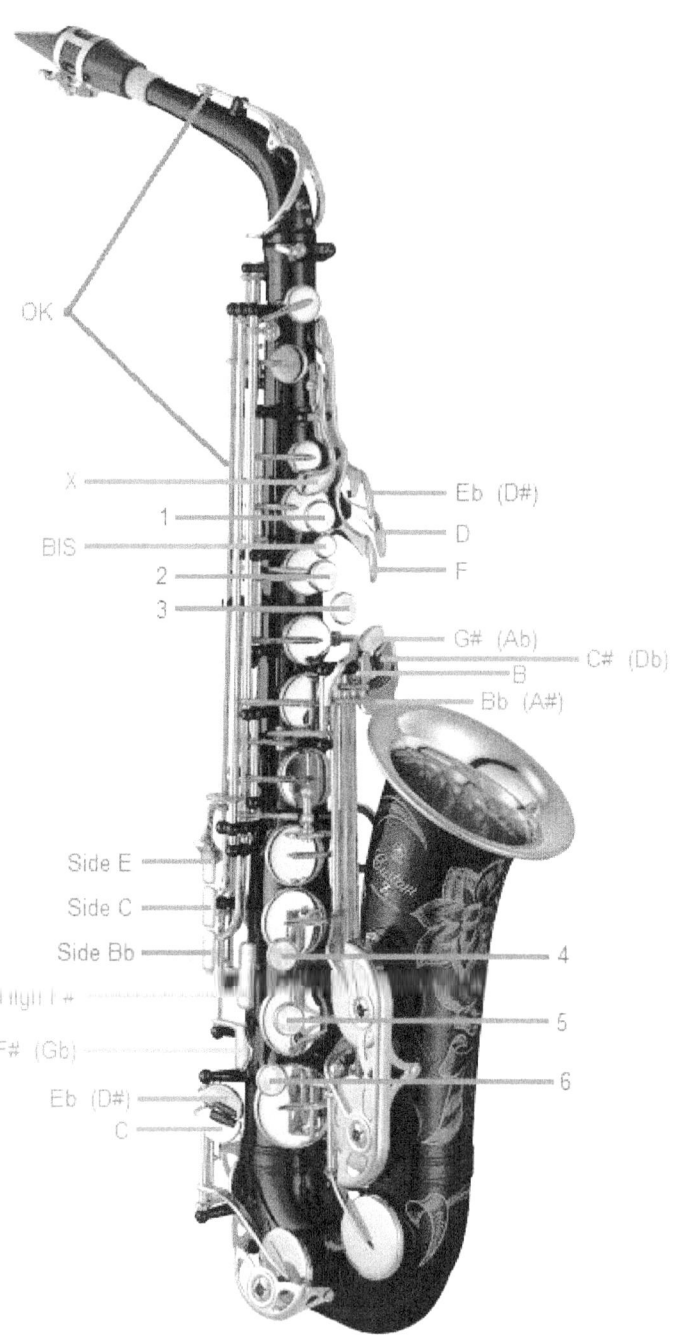

SIMPLE TO PLAY

The entire system becomes simple when you understand which finger goes where.

Top Notes

You play the top notes using the left hand. This is the Octave Key, and there is a thumb rest below it that you can press when needed.

The next key is X, which helps you with alternate fingering. After that is the key marked 1; use your index finger to play this. The next key is 2, played by the middle finger and the next key, marked 3, is for your third finger.

Below this, you see a cluster of 4 notes. Use your pinky to press all these keys.

Top Side Keys

Use the palm of your right hand (below the index finger) to press the side D key. Use the index finger to press the Eb key, and for the F key, use your third finger. These are the four or five rectangular keys. On the top left-hand side, you find the three palm keys. They have this name because you can play them with your palm. These two sets of notes play high notes and trills, and along with the front F key, are spatula keys or spatulas. Keys with a lever-action are called levers.

Right-Hand Bottom Notes

Use the index finger for the key marked 4 and the middle finger to play the key marked 5. The key marked 6 is for your third finger. Below these, you will find two half-moon shaped keys which you play using your pinky.

Bottom Side Keys

You use your index finger to play all three side keys Bb, C, and E. Use the third finger to press the side F# key.

Little Finger Keys

The little finger keys also have the names touch plates or table keys. The group of two keys for the right hand has the name lower stack, and the group of four for the left hand we call the upper stack. We also refer to them as clusters, plateaus, and (floating rocker) tables.

Unlike the piano, where each key has a specific name, the saxophone's keys do not. This is because each note needs a combination of keys. It is useful to identify the keys.

Keys 1 to 8

You play the keys 1 to 6 with the left and right index, ring, and middle fingers. Use your little finger to play key 7: the low C and the low Eb key. Operate key 8 on the lower stack using your left little finger.

Octave Key

Key O is on the back. Let us say you play a low G and then press the octave key. The note you hear will now have the G note an octave higher. The octave key opens and closes two vents. You can see the upper one on the neck. We have the lower octave vent on the body between the F# and high E key cups. You need not worry about which one to use because when you play the octave key, the saxophone automatically opens the right vent.

The Highest Notes

The highest notes are keys C1 to C5. As the number increases, the pitch of the note also climbs up. C5 is for the high F# (F sharp) but you will not find this on all saxophones.

Trills and More

We use the keys that have a T mark to play trills, but that is not all. Suppose we consider Tc; we can also play C. For trilling, you can do:

Tc - trill between B and C.

Tf - trill between F and F#.

Ta - trill between A and Bb.

F=X

We call the Key X forked F, quick F, or front F. With this, you can reach the high F, high E, and F#.

Fingering Charts

You can play notes using fingering charts as they show you the exact combination of keys to play a note.

The Registers

We call the octave key the register key. While playing the lowest series of keys (low register), you use this key to go to the next series (the middle series) that sounds higher.

Three Registers

Saxophonists group the instrument range into low, middle, and upper registers. When you don't use the octave key, you are in the lower register. When you use the register key, you are in the middle register and adding keys C1 to C5 gets you to the upper register.

Five Registers

Many other players say there are five registers. Here the bottom register refers to the lowest four notes - Bb, B, C, C#. Using the octave key differentiates the lower and upper key since both need the same six pearl keys and we use top notes (C1 to C5) or harmonics to play the very highest notes in the altissimo register, requiring changes to the air stream and special fingering.

CHAPTER 2

THE FOUR SAXES

When you go to buy a saxophone, they will ask you which one you want - an Alto, Tenor, a Baritone, or a Soprano. These are the four voices. You must learn their sound and ranges, and when C is not a C. As a generality, a baritone sax is bigger and lower sounding in tone than the rest.

SOPRANO

The high-sounding soprano is the easiest to handle because of its size. But beginners must avoid sopranos because smaller horns are harder to play than tenors or altos. Sopranos have a straight body in most cases, but you can also get curved sopranos.

ALTO

The alto sax is the best choice for beginners. Playing an alto in tune is easier than playing a soprano and easier to handle than a tenor. There is plenty of classical music written for alto because it is more compatible with all music and remains a popular choice in marching bands and concerts.

TENOR

The tenor is famous for its use in jazz music, but it has a place in most other genres as well. The sound is juicier, richer, or warmer than alto or soprano, and it is more versatile. You can make the tenor saxophone sound like a piercing cry and edgy or soft as a whisper. For the beginner, this is the best choice, along with the alto sax.

BARITONE

This is the biggest one of them all, but it is far harder to manage. As such, it has a looped neck along with a tall bell. If this were not so, the baritone sax would be over seven feet tall. The big fat tone of the baritone is one octave lower than the alto. It is not good for beginners because it is costly and has an enormous size.

HOW HIGH TO GO?

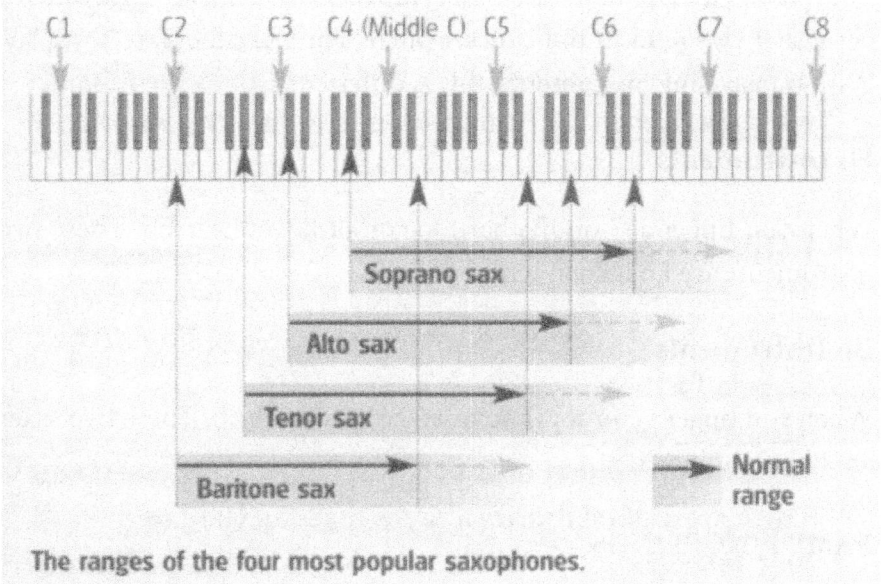

The ranges of the four most popular saxophones.

The normal range of the saxophone is two-and-a-half octaves. Talented players will stretch this to three of four octaves or even more.

Same Note with Different Timbre

You will see at least fourteen notes you can play on all four saxophones. It begins from Ab below middle C (Ab3), up to next A (A4). These fourteen notes voices will sound different for each sax because of the change in timbre.

Transposing Instruments

If you see C on the chart and play it on a piano, you hear C. If the saxophone chart shows C and you finger C, you will hear another note. This is because the saxophone is a transposing instrument.

Concert Instruments

The piano, guitar, and other instruments are concert instruments because they sound in the concert pitch. You hear the note you play. With transposing instruments, this is different.

Eb Instruments

When you finger a C on the baritone or alto, you hear Eb. These two instruments are Eb instruments.

Bb Instruments

When you finger C on soprano or tenor, you hear Bb. These two saxes are Bb instruments.

Same Fingerings

Though it is confusing at first, the fact remains that no matter which sax you play, the fingerings remain the same. For instance, middle C on paper means you are close to six pearl keys plus key 7 (right little finger). The note that comes out is the note the composer wants to hear.

Here is the note C5 on paper and the corresponding C for all saxes and the resulting concert pitches.

TRANSPOSED PARTS

The saxophonist's part does not tell you which pitch to play but which notes to finger. Saxophonists read transposed parts. When you play your part, your instrument transposes the written note to the pitch the composer has in mind. If you are playing alto and the composer wants to concert Eb, you will find C on your part. If the composer wants the tenor to sound an Eb, he will have to play an E.

SAXOPHONES IN C

Why is there so much mix-up? Will it not become simple if all saxophones sound in C like a piano? Yes, but changing the saxophone tuning will also change its timbre. What would happen is that the tenor saxophone in C would be smaller than the tenor in Bb. Because of this small size, the sound will tend towards an alto.

ALTO IN C

An alto couldn't sound the note C. To do this, it would have to be smaller than a soprano or as big as a tenor. The fact is that they have made saxophones in C. But the Eb and Bb instruments are more popular.

OTHER WIND INSTRUMENTS

There are other transposing instruments besides the sax. For instance, there are trumpets and clarinets in Bb like the tenor and soprano saxes and alto flutes in G. There are French horns in F and Bb.

LEARNING TO PLAY

It is easy to learn to play the saxophone, but to learn to play it well will take time, especially learning to play it in tune and producing a decent sound from it. Here we see the key elements comprising learning the instrument, practicing, and lessons.

Good Sound

It will take a long time to make the saxophone sound the way you want it to sound. The instrument will only sound as perfect as the player and his or her skill.

The first thing to understand is that it takes more than merely blowing air through a hole to play the instrument. To make a wonderful sound, you need to have superb breath control. Having good air stream control allows you to play in tune and play long phrases.

Embouchure

The next important thing to learn is how to shape your lips, tongue, and jaws. You must have control over all the surrounding muscles.

Taken together, this is the embouchure. The basis for this word is bouche, the French word for mouth.

LESSONS

A good teacher will show you everything there is to do with the instrument. You begin with developing air control with the embouchure and proceeding to play in tune. You will also learn to read music and maintain a good posture.

Locate an Excellent Teacher

Music stores have teachers on their panel. If you contact them, they will direct you to one or you could check at your school to find one. We can see the classified ads in newspapers and music magazines. Also, check the supermarket bulletin boards and the Yellow Pages. Professional private teachers charge between twenty-five and seventy-five dollars per hour. If you want them to make house calls, it will cost extra.

You can opt for group lessons instead of private lessons. This will work out cheaper, though you will miss on the private attention. If you want to learn fast, take private lessons.

Check the Collectives

If you check the music schools and collectives in your locality, you will get extras such as ensemble playing, clinics, and master classes. You will get exposure to a variety of styles and see players perform at various levels.

QUESTIONS TO ASK YOUR TEACHER

The first obvious question is how much it is going to cost you. Apart from that, here are some more questions to ask:

- Do you get a free introductory class? This class shows you how good the teacher is and whether you will get along with the teacher.
- Will the teacher expect you to put in a lot of practice? Will he allow you to learn if you are only there for the fun of it?
- Is there course material provided? Does the student have to invest in method books?
- Do they allow you to record your sessions so you can listen at home? This way you can go through the lessons at your leisure.
- Will you have the option of choosing a specific style of play? Or will you have to learn a lot of styles?
- Will the teacher make you practice scales for two years? Will I get to perform soon?

Once you know the answer to all these questions, you can decide whether this teacher is the one you want.

PRACTICING

Any student learning an instrument will have to practice. It is better to play one hour every day instead of three hours once a week. Practicing the embouchure daily helps you get used to the style.

Break it Up

If you find it hard to play for half an hour straight without letting up, use brief spells of ten minutes through the duration of the day. Work your way up to 15 minutes and then 20 minutes, and so on.

Getting the Right Sound

When you finger the notes on the saxophone, they will not sound in pitch right away. You will find they sound flat when you take it easy and shrill when you put in too much effort. So, to play the instrument in the right pitch, learn to use your embouchure and control the air stream. The more you play, the better you get at listening to play the right pitch.

Neighbors

Since the instrument's sound will carry for quite some distance, you will need a proper room to begin your practice. People in the house also might get disturbed by your sax practice. Consider soundproofing the room or go somewhere else to practice. Muting with towels in the bell might work if you play only the mid-range notes. The top notes will not sound, and the lowest ones will get muffled too much.

The best alternative is to use a bag that completely covers the instrument. It will have three openings - one for the mouthpiece and one each for each hand. During practice, consider covering your ears using earmuffs or earplugs. You are playing in a confined space and playing loud as well. When you cover your ears, it will sound as though the sax is next door. Check out ear protectors that have adjustable filters.

Play-Along CDs

It is good to practice with others but check the play-along CDs if you don't have company. You can get CDs for specific styles, for beginners, and the experts. Specialized CDs will have your part left out so you can fill in with your practice. If you have a computer, use special CD ROMs to practice. Some feature entire orchestras and allow you to decide how fast you want to play.

Start by selecting the piece you want to play. Some software allows you to slow down the tempo of tough pieces. Practicing with the metronome, a small mechanical device that provides a steady tick-tock at your chosen speed, helps you maintain a steady beat at all times. You can also purchase digital metronomes.

Record Your Sessions

If you record your session, you can listen to the teacher's instructions again and you will hear what you sounded like during the practice session. This will help you correct your mistakes and become a better player. Most professionals use this kind of recording to improve their technique.

You will need a cassette recorder with a built-in microphone, preferably a high-quality one for better playback. Also, make it a point to visit music concerts, festivals, and shows to learn about different styles and techniques for playing the instrument.

CHAPTER 3

BUYING A SAXOPHONE

The sax is not a cheap instrument because it has complicated key work, but it is possible to get the best instruments at a low price. Here you can read about selecting the best instrument and whether you should go for a second-hand instrument.

The reason a sax costs so much is that it takes considerable time to make one. A basic new alto sax can easily cost a thousand dollars. Professional altos begin at three thousand dollars but you can get one with the professional label for a lower price. The expensive altos are twice this price or even more. Tenors have a price that is five to ten percent more.

SOPRANOS AND BARITONES

When you have saxes of the same quality, the soprano costs more than the tenor or alto. The soprano is small, and it is more difficult to make one that plays well and remains in tune. Baritones are costly because of their vast size and also because they make so few of them. Prices begin at two thousand and go up to seven.

To the casual viewer, the ordinary sax looks the same as a professional one. To hear the difference, you need to have the skills to play it better. This means that you are better off playing a student sax for a couple of years until you can play at a higher level.

TIME AND EFFORT

You might ask, why pay more? Expensive saxes have more effort and time put into them. The material used is also terrific, and they have a better mechanism, with stronger rods and better springs. You have adjustable keys and ornamental engravings with silver and gold plating instead of a lacquer finish. Making them requires more handiwork and development and research.

A Better Sound

So, you get a better sound from an expensive horn and the instrument is reliable and easy to play. It stays in tune for a longer period compared to a budget instrument and you have better resale value for a high-quality instrument.

Money for Reeds and Maintenance

When you invest in an instrument, you will need some more money for the reeds and maintenance. Your instrument might also need a better neck or mouthpiece.

THE MUSIC SHOP

The saxophone is a high-precision instrument that needs periodic maintenance and tuning. Even when new, they need proper tuning and adjustment. If the shop has trained musicians on the staff, they will help you when you buy the instrument. The trained staff will not send you home with a poorly adjusted instrument.

For the maintenance, every sax needs its COA - cleaning, oiling, and adjustment. The first-time service might be free for a new instrument. When you buy an instrument, visit a few stores to compare the price and quality. Also, not all shops will have all the brands. Take plenty of time to select the instrument. In a few shops, they have a testing room to check how well your instrument plays and some allow you to take the instrument home to check it at your leisure. It is more common with pro-level saxes than with the common ones. Remember, no two saxes sound the same and the same goes with the mouthpiece as well. It is a common practice to take an expert player with you because he can tell you how responsive the instrument is and how true it sounds.

Buying and Renting Online

There are many online stores where you can buy a saxophone. You can check it in your house and send it back within a stipulated time if you don't like it. A few stores allow you to rent the instrument. It costs between $25-$50 a month, and you have to pay for at least three months in advance. The rental fee will depend on the retail price of the instrument. So, if you select a high-priced instrument, expect to pay more rent for it. If you rent a used instrument, the rent will be lower. The store might want your credit card details or ask for a deposit.

Buying It

A few shops offer you the rent-to-own program. Here, they deduct all (or a small part) of the rental fees you pay if you decide to buy the instrument. Or they might offer you a discount on a new instrument if you regularly rent from the shop. If you have rented for a longer time, the discount is more. Always check the contract before you sign your rental agreement to see if there is any offer or pre-condition included.

SECOND-HAND INSTRUMENTS

You might think second-hand instruments are cheaper, but this is not always the case. A decent used instrument can cost as much as a student sax. It is also possible to get used models made thirty years ago at a lower price than the regular student's model.

Overhaul

Before they sell you a second-hand instrument, they will overhaul it. If there are loose and broken parts, they get replaced.

Beginners Models and Vintage Horns

Vintage horns are the favorites for jazz players. The sound is fatter and richer than that of instruments made during the past few years. Beginners can play with vintage horns if you can find one for a lower price. You can get second-hand saxes at private music stores or check the newspaper for ads, and you might get one cheap. Though you may get one for a low price, not all vintage horns are easy to play. Also, being vintage does not make it a suitable instrument to play and beginners should really be looking for an instrument that is easy to play.

CHOOSE A PLACE TO BUY

Check out the classified section of the newspapers for some good deals on saxophones. You can also get second-hand instruments from private music stores. See if you can get them on the internet. By comparing the notices, it is possible to get one for a low price.

From a Music Store

There are advantages to buying it from a music store. The instrument may have undergone checks, it may have been adjusted so it has a perfect tone, and it might have a warranty. You can go also take it back if there are any doubts. You get to choose from a large number and variety of instruments by checking them one by one.

You get to see the actual color and shape and have an accurate idea of the size. When you buy online, this much information is not available. If your store is good, they will not overcharge you. Private sellers will because they think you don't know better or because they don't.

Get a Second Opinion

Even when you are confident about how the instrument should be, it never hurts to ask another person. Take along with you a person experienced at playing the saxophone. He might tell you something you have overlooked. If you are buying from a private seller, you might overlook a perfectly good saxophone because it doesn't look good. Or you might buy one that looks great but is bad.

A Good Saxophone

Saxophones all look alike superficially. This goes for all tenor and alto saxophones. Yet, each one is different and has a different body. Some have extra keys and special features. Here we see what these differences are, along with tips to play each instrument.

The first and most important aspect comprises the mouthpiece and reed. We will see this in more detail in the coming chapter.

Why do two identical saxophones sound different? And why does the same sax make a unique sound when played by a different player? This is because every sax has a unique body and finish.

Tips for the Traveling Saxophonist

Sometimes you are in trouble, and there is no technician around to help you. Here are a few things you can do.

- **Key Stops Working** - The fault may lie with the spring. Check the spring to see if it has broken. If it is, use a rubber band. It will hold out fine until you get to a repair shop.

- **Book Seats in the Back of the Airplane** - You will need overhead space when you board the plane. Most plane boarding starts from the rear end, so it increases your chances if you book your seat at the back.

- **Buy a Compact Case** - Buy a suitable case molded in the horn's shape and avoid soft gig bags. If someone tries to squeeze their luggage against your horn, the soft bags will offer no protection.

- **The G# Key isn't Working** - When you press the G# key, it doesn't work. This key is notorious for sticking on all saxes, and it is easy to fix it. First, locate the G# key and pull it. Once it is open, prevent it from sticking using a piece of paper or a dollar bill. Powder paper works longer. You might face a problem with the spring mechanism but, even though you may be able to fix it, let a mechanic or your teacher fix it.

- **Low Notes are Not Working** - There are two or three reasons for this to happen. Check which low notes are not working. If the low C, B, and Bb are not working but the notes from D to F work, the problem is with the low notes' pads. These probably fell out of alignment or are torn or dried up. Again, it is better to let a repairman fix it. You need to reseat the pads, so they are back in place and sealing the hole properly. Ask your teacher to show you how to use a leak light to solve this problem permanently.

- **Keys Below G** - When the notes below G are not working well, it is probably a loose screw on the G# key.

- **Middle D Doesn't Come Out Right** - You play the middle D by playing the low D with the octave key. If there is a problem, it must concern the octave key mechanism. If it has a fuzzy sound or overblow to high-A, then it is time to fix it and you can even do it yourself. The octave mechanism is on the neck of the saxophone. When you play the notes from the middle D to high G, the mechanism on the neck opens a little. If you play the high-A, it opens some more. If you bend the mechanism back into place, the problem gets solved. It happens when you are not careful while taking or putting back the instrument from its case. It depends on how delicate your sax is.

- **Keys Make a Lot of Noise** - This may not seem to be a problem with some players. When you are only practicing, the extra noise will not trouble you. You will not get disturbed by the noise that you don't hear, anyway. But if you are recording or giving a performance, this will need correction because the microphone will pick up the extra noise. The solution is to get the sax repaired by a repairman. Oil the keys and replace old and missing felts and corks. This will reduce the extra noise.

- **Some Other Key is Not Working** - Let the teacher have a look at it. There are many mechanisms, and cheaper saxes have more problems. If you cannot fix it, take the instrument to a repairman.

- **Air Leaks** - As mentioned above, if the leak is too big, the note will not play at all. The reason is that of the age of the saxophone. The leather gets stiff and stops sealing the hole as it should.

- **Problem with the Neck Cork** - This is easy to spot since it looks like a wine cork between the neck and the mouthpiece. We use the neck cork to make sure there is no air leak, and it can be replaced if it breaks or leaks. In normal play, the cork compresses and comes loose, and this is nothing to get alarmed about. When the technician replaces the cork, he cuts the new cork to fit and glues it into place. He shapes the cork, so it holds the mouthpiece tight. It is not a costly repair, and when done properly, it will hold out for a few years.

- **There are Dents** - Because of the soft nature of the saxophone's material, we can expect a couple of dents in time. In this matter, you can let the repairman do the work because you are likely to cause more damage than good. Choose the technician with experience in this line of work.

- **Reattach Fallen Key Pearl** - If you have a cheap saxophone, a key pearl has likely fallen off. Use one tiny drop of glue to fix it back into place.

- **Neck Tenon is Loose** - If the neck tenon does not have a good fit, you must take care of it. Use 1200 grit sandpaper and cut a small piece. It should be a little longer than the tenon. Wrap the piece around the tenon using slow twisting movements. This will smooth out any rough spots on the tenon. It will have a snugger fit now.

CHAPTER 4

THE BODY

The exact dimensions of the saxophone's body are more important than anything else for gauging the sound and the body material is also important.

BRASS

Almost all saxophones are yellow brass instruments, although some show a distinctive red shade because of the excess presence of copper. They have 85% copper compared to the normal 70% and a few experts say this is the reason for the warm sound, while others say the sound is bright.

SOLID SILVER OR GOLD

A solid silver body produces a crisp, wholesome sound with more projection and clarity. Some say the sax has more power, but the detractors say the opposite. Remember, opinions remain layered by the ability to express feelings and their individual experience with playing the sax. Solid gold saxes are rare and said to have a very warm, homogeneous, and round sound.

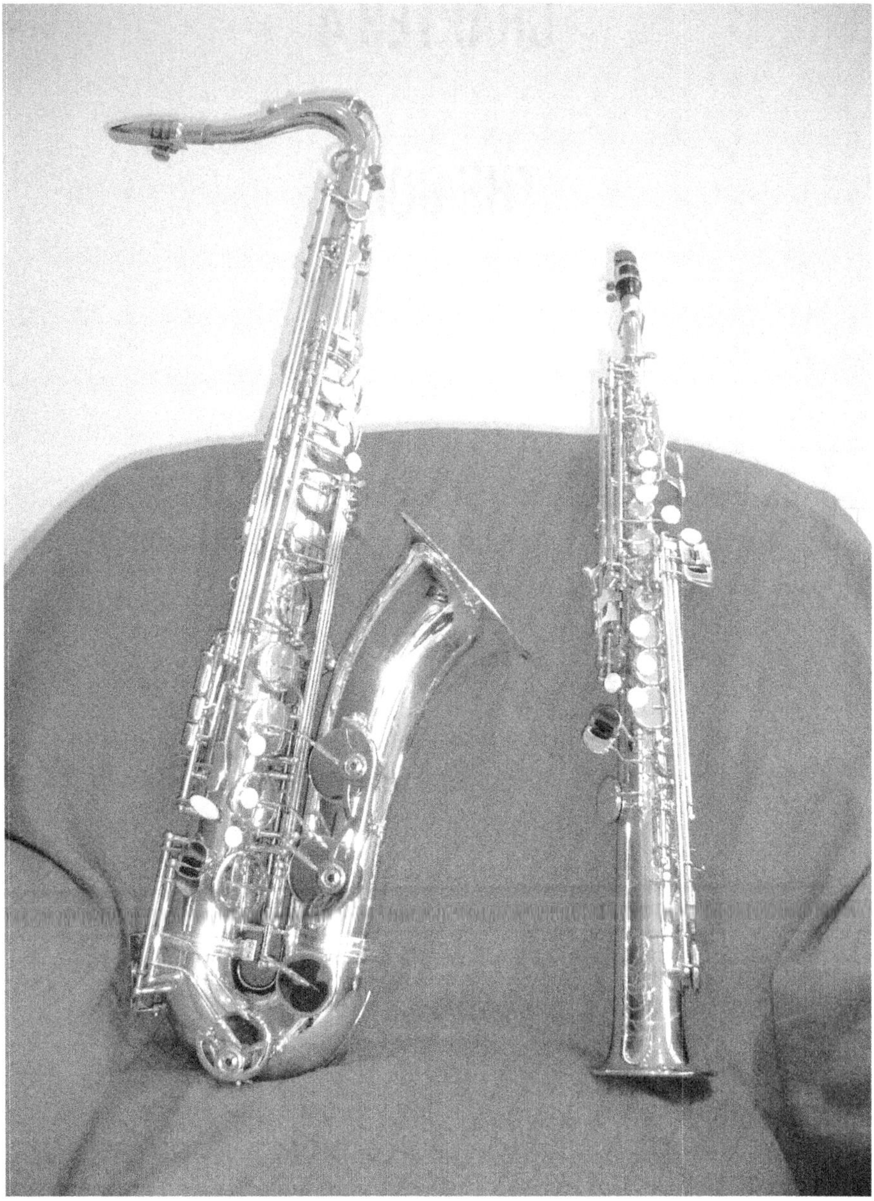

THE BORE

When you play the sax, the air column inside it vibrates and the bore, the actual inner diameter of the body, affects the timbre. Vintage instruments sound the way they do because of a thinner bore and the smaller bore also makes it harder to play.

COMPARISON

Other than that, there isn't much to tell them apart. The inner dimension is conical from top to tip, making it difficult to measure with any accuracy, which is probably why so little has been written on this topic. We can read about alloys, finishes, and sizes, but not the volume or its measurements.

CURVED AND STRAIGHT SOPRANOS

Traditional Sopranos have a straight body. You can get a few brands that offer a curved body because they have a fuller and rounder sound. It has a softness that makes the timbre true.

STRAIGHT AND CURVED NECKS

Many Sopranos in the upper price range come with both a straight and a curved neck. We can describe the sounds produced by the curved and straight neck saxes in similar words.

Curved necks have a dark and warm sound with a milder tone. In comparison, straight Sopranos have a brighter sound, and the tone is edgier.

Another construction while choosing the neck is the ease of use. To have the mouthpiece at the needed angle, hold the straight soprano with a straight neck close to horizontal. When we consider the curved soprano, it is comfortable and has a comfortable feel about it.

Some experts think the straight soprano saxophone has a better intonation, meaning they are easier to play in tune. In fact, sopranos are harder to play than the larger saxes. Another reason the saxophonists prefer curved sopranos is that they can hear themselves better, because the bell doesn't point away from the user.

There are a few Saxophone manufacturers that make straight tenors and altos, and the same rules apply to them.

THE NECK

This part has a dominant effect on the sound because it is closer to the mouth. Often, we find altos and tenors with two necks, both with different finishes and bores. They make one with a mellow tone while the other has a brighter sound and you can swap necks to change the acoustics of the sax. This becomes necessary when you play at a venue with altered interiors that deflect sound differently.

THE DESIGN OF THE MOUTHPIECE

The factors that matter in the mouthpiece's design include considerations of shape and size because the dimensions affect the pitch, tone quality, equality of registers, volume, ease of playing, and flexibility. One should have enough knowledge about how each factor affects the quality of tone production before selecting the mouthpiece. Within the inner chamber of the mouthpiece, we see the birth of the tone's quality. The mouthpiece and reed both act as generating mechanisms. This mechanism sets up the fundamental tone and establishes the way each parameter affects the partials. Here, one should know about medium facing.

In the most general case, this term defines the setting under which the saxophonist gets the best result. We use trial and error to determine this, but it need not be the best value. It becomes the starting point for the musician who wishes to get the best result and a variety of factors control the performance of the mouthpiece, including:

- **The Facing:** The major influence comes from the shape of the curve, leaving the mouthpiece's flat table. Tip opening is the distance between the reed and the mouthpiece tip, and it depends on the extent of the curve. A long facing will induce biting, as we have to exert more force to close the gap up to where it vibrates. You need a softer bite and a shorter reed, which weakens the high notes, while a short facing reduces the control of the embouchure and its flexibility. Tones now become thin and low tones start breaking. There is no pressure on the embouchure, but the dynamic range gets reduced. Soft playing becomes difficult because of the wide tip opening and the coarse tone gives a false sense of volume. Unless you have enough power in the embouchure muscles, you will need a soft reed.

- Using the narrow tip for the narrow tip opening results in a thin tone and the high register becomes sharp. We see the general opinion is that the curve of the facing must remain as the arc of a perfect circle and in the chapter on reeds, you see the scientific evidence for this. It shows that the reed will close the tip opening. According to this principle, we will see that we can produce an infinite number of facings by moving the axis of the arc.

- **The Baffle:** It is the part of the mouthpiece directly behind the tip, receiving the vibration's first shock as it leaves the reed. A high baffle leaves a brief space between the mouthpiece and the reed. This reinforces the upper partials and creates a buzz or edge to the sound, but it might cause squeaks and tone production, though good, remains rough. A low baffle produces a dead, dark sound that lacks carrying power, creating a distance that remains close to the reed tip and making it hard to blow.

- **The Tip Rail**: We can describe the broad rail as a defensive device. Though it is excellent for soft playing, it is not capable of any projection. The sound it emits is pure but with the absence of higher partials. So, it has no edgy quality but lacks flexibility. The narrow rail is best avoided as it causes squeaks and chirps. The reed must be a perfect fit.

CHAPTER 5

PARTS OF THE SAXOPHONE

Assemble the Saxophone

Though the saxophone has rugged parts, it is easy to bend the side keys, connecting levers, and long rods out of line if one is not careful. Make sure you do not force the rods or keys when you assemble the instrument. Before you begin, make sure you have lubricated the cork well. You find it on the neck of the instrument. Use plenty of cork grease. Here are the steps for beginners to follow:

1. Begin with the neck strap. Take it out of the case and put it around your neck. Look at the device that adjusts the length and become familiar with its working.

2. Take hold of the bell of the instrument without touching the keys. Hook the neck strap onto the body of the saxophone. There is an end cover for the lever connecting to the octave key. Remove it.

3. Make sure the tension screw that keeps the neck in position is loose. Make sure that the end of the body itself and the sleeve that fits the body is clean. When there is difficulty fitting the

instrument's body to the neck, use Vaseline or grease to lubricate the neck.

4. Hold the neck in the right palm and hold down the octave key.

5. Hold the instrument's body with the left hand and push it on to the neck. Make sure you do not bend the connecting lever. This happens when you turn the neck at an awkward angle.

6. Keep the brace at the bottom of the neck in line with the instrument body's connecting lever. Tighten the tension screw so that the neck is well in place.

7. Remove the ligature and reed from the mouthpiece. Use the right palm to hold the mouthpiece and keep the left hand on the neck; the palm must hold down the octave key. The neck strap takes the weight of the instrument.

8. Place the mouthpiece so that at least half of the cork remains covered. The exact distance will get set during the tuning process.

9. Along with the cork, if there is a tuning screw on the neck, push the mouthpiece to cover the entire cork.

ADJUST THE LIGATURE AND REED

You must take care not to chip the tip of the reed. For this, place the ligature first around the mouthpiece. Now, slip the reed down inside it. The mouthpiece has a flat part called the lay and the reed will come exactly in its center. Make sure the reed is well-centered by checking the tip and butt end. When looking down at the reed tip from the mouthpiece's tip, a sixty-fourth inch of the mouthpiece will remain visible. After placing the reed well, locate the ligature and place it, so its edges are in the mouthpiece's marking.

Tighten the screws so that the reed stays in place. You must only tighten the ligature until the reed is well in place. To get proper control of the sound production and tone, you must place the ligature and reed properly. Practice placing the ligature and reed daily to achieve fluency.

SAXOPHONE POSITION

1. Hold the saxophone to the right of your body and rest the instrument against the side of your leg. The instrument remains vertical, and its bottom is further back. Keep the right arm relaxed and push the elbow back a little. This gives your right hand its best playing position.

2. The weight of the instrument will remain on the neck strap and you use your right and left thumbs to balance it. Adjust the length of the neck strap so that the center of your lower lip touches the mouthpiece.

3. Use the flesh and the base of the nail of the right thumb to contact the thumb rest. The ball of the thumb is on the instrument's body, in contact with the pearl buttons of the tone holes. Establish a guide position by keeping all the fingers in position. You must maintain this all the time. Check the guide position often until it becomes automatic.

4. Use the left thumb to operate the octave key. Place it diagonally across the instrument body with the fleshy part of the ball remaining on the plate given for it. The tip of the finger will touch but not press the octave key. You can control the octave key with a vertical movement of the first joint of the thumb.

5. In the guide position, the remaining fingers fall into a natural curve without tension. The left little finger touches the G# (G sharp) key lightly, while the right little finger will touch the C key.

Form the Embouchure

Follow the directions from your music instructor while forming the embouchure. You can use the method outlined below until you reach the right standard. Check in the mirror to see whether you have achieved the right formation.

1. Start with your lips pressed tight against each other and bring the lower jaw down to create a gap three-eighths of an inch in size.

2. Say the word O so that the lips take a curved shape. You get slight wrinkles around your lips.

3. Keep your teeth parted and lips curved. Bring the rim of the lower lip over the top edge of the front teeth. Use your finger to feel this or lower and raise your jaw until you get the right position.

4. Using this position, insert the saxophone mouthpiece inside the mouth and allow the reed to push your lower lip into the teeth. Maintain the lower lip's wrinkles and keep the line dividing the lip from the chin over the front edge of the lower teeth. If the student has thick lips, they must adjust to make the lip go over the teeth less.

5. Turn the corner of the mouth and lips so that no air can escape.

6. To allow free vibration, free the end of the reed from any form of contact. It is three-eighths to half an inch for the alto saxophone and more for the tenor. The length of the mouthpiece to remain in the mouth will depend on the mouthpiece itself.

7. Rest the upper teeth but do not press on the top of the mouthpiece. This will remain a little in front of the lower teeth.

Keep the lower teeth in an open position. But do not bite or exert pressure on the lower lip.

8. Control and support the mouthpiece and reed with an inward pressure towards the mouthpiece center using the lips and the corner of the mouth.

Tone production is as follows below.

BASIC TONE PRODUCTION

Before you attempt to make a sound with the instrument, use the mouthpiece alone to get the tone correct.

1. Select a reed and place it in the mouthpiece in the proper place. Adjust the ligature.
2. Make the embouchure and check in the mirror to see whether you got the right shape.
3. Use the support of the abdominal breath to produce a tone. Make sure you are using the embouchure formation properly.
4. Practice until you can make a steady tone of the highest pitch. You must maintain it for 10 seconds at least.
5. When you can do this, you can practice the exercises.

TAKE CARE OF THE INSTRUMENT

You must dry the instrument thoroughly after use and then put it into its case. Dissemble occurs in the reverse order of assemble. The saxophone has a swab you can use to clean the inside of the body of the instrument. To clean the inside of the neck, a special neck cleaner is used. Make sure the body of the instrument has no fingerprints. If there is any dust beneath the key mechanism, you can remove it using a soft watercolor brush.

Oiling of the mechanism is necessary three to four times a year. You get a key oil from the market. Use a drop of oil on the end of the nail (or toothpick) on each pivot screw of each key. Dry the mouthpiece after you remove the reed using a soft cloth or chamois. Keep reeds in the reed holder or case made especially for this. If you leave the reeds without care, they will soon get damaged beyond use. Put all the instrument parts into the case, making sure you replace the plug on the small side of the body. Here, we have small compartments in which you can place the neck strap, neck, reed case, ligature, and mouthpiece. Do not force the case to close.

Lubricate the neck cork well using cork grease as also the sleeve and its connecting part to the body. Make sure they are clean before lubricating.

Keep the instrument in a place where there is no direct sunlight or heat source.

INTONATION AND TUNING

Since saxophones are transposing instruments, you need to play the F# on the alto saxophone and B on the tenor saxophone to get A-440 standard pitch. In bands, they often play B-flat (Bb) as the tuning note for which they play the G-natural (G) on the alto saxophone. The tenor saxophone plays C natural (C), and they tune the instrument using the mouthpiece. If they get a flat tone, they push the mouthpiece further on the cork. If the tone is sharp, they pull the mouthpiece, so less cork remains covered. The accepted tuning is A-440, and all saxophones must remain tuned to this. This is when approximately half the cork remains covered.

The saxophone might have a tuning screw on its neck instead of a long cork. Now, the mouthpiece comes over the entire cork, and you tune it using the screw.

The intonation of the saxophone depends on many things:

a) How the instrument is made.

b) The embouchure is well-formed and developed.

c) The mouthpiece fits the instrument well, and the design of the tone chamber is correct.

d) A well-adjusted reed that fits both the mouthpiece and embouchure.

You will find all the recognized brands of saxophones are well-tuned. We can play them in tune when other things remain right. You will see the instrument sounds sharp if we set the reed hard, and if it is too soft, the instrument will sound flat. The primary controlling factor in intonation is embouchure. The amount of mouthpiece in the mouth is also critical. If it is too little, the higher notes will sound flat while too much will make all the notes sound flat. Also, when there is too much mouthpiece, it becomes impossible to control the individual notes. Complications also arise when you bite with the lower teeth. Change the angle at which you hold the instrument to improve the control the embouchure has. Any standard brand's mouthpiece should have the reed and embouchure in good shape before you determine any problem.

WOODWIND GUIDE

Here we are going to discuss how to play the alto saxophone because it is the most widely used instrument. We will also discuss special problems associated with it as different from other instruments. The theoretical written range remains the same for all instruments except the Bass and Soprano, which do not have the lowest two notes. Each instrument has its sounding range and remains as transposing instruments.

B-flat Soprano: It sounds a whole step lower than what we write. A soprano saxophone in C, we find occasionally sounding the pitch is the same as a written note. One such instrument is the C-melody saxophone. Now it is obsolete, but a student might bring one home by mistake because it resembles the B-flat tenor instrument. After all, they both look alike. When this happens, the teacher has to explain in considerable length why we cannot use it. In the band or a beginner's class, there is no music written for it.

RANGES

The saxophone's acoustics lends itself to improving the playing range of the student to a large extent within a few days. While playing the instrument, we do not use the baritone and tenor instruments' top notes, unlike alto. One can extend the playing range beyond the standard high F if the student has skills on the alto and to a lesser extent on the tenor.

- E-flat Alto: Sound is a major sixth lower than what we write.
- B-flat Tenor: Sound is a major ninth lower than what we write.
- E-flat Baritone: Sound is an octave plus a major sixth lower compared to what we write.
- B-flat Bass (rarely found): Sound is two full octaves plus a whole step lower than what we write.

The saxophone parts are a mouthpiece, ligature, body, neck, mouthpiece cap, neck strap, and reed. They only differ in size according to which instrument you pick. The Soprano is normally straight in one single unit comprising the body and neck.

It is hard to find the perfect mouthpiece for any woodwind instrument. There is no one-solution-fits-all available. The aim of the sax player must be to make a start in the right direction. At one end of the scale, we have the mouthpiece-itis sufferer who wastes time changing the mouthpiece rather than playing the instrument. At the other end, we see the person afraid to change or try something new. The approach to the problem lies between these two opposing points.

There are a few things that prevent the use of identical mouthpieces for all instruments. These include:

1. The need to fit the shape and musculature of the face.
2. Changed shape of the teeth.
3. Structure of the bones of the face.
4. Thickness and size of the lips.

You can add to these the many playing styles, individual tonal concepts, and the demands of different engagements. Despite the confusion, physical principles remain involved that includes the selection of the mouthpiece for the individual. The mouthpiece supplied as standard should prove enough for the beginner. That is until the student exerts his individuality.

The beginner's mouthpiece, in normal cases, is chamber and medium facing. If you need anything else, the teacher can help with this. New students should not keep running to the music store to buy a new one without enough reason, such as problems in the facing and make. Many people waste their money on models of a different color or different material, having a fancy shape, or things like that and this often proves wrong for the individual.

Another beginner's mistake is buying a mouthpiece or facing because some famous personality uses it. The mouthpiece plays an important role in the embouchure's formation, so one must not take it casually. It is not something your aunt must buy you for Christmas unless she has the advice of an expert who has enough knowledge on its use.

CHAPTER 6

THE SAXOPHONE MOUTHPIECE

The mouthpiece of the saxophone is metal, glass, ebonite, or plastic and each has an original property, depending on the manufacturer. The individual can choose the material he likes. If the mouthpiece's dimensions are the same (including the outside measurements and the chamber), they will sound similar and a casual listener cannot tell the difference when one uses a different mouthpiece. The choice of the material has a psychological effect on the user and depends on the material.

Finding a glass mouthpiece is rare, though many clarinetists use one for their performances. Being fragile, a slight bump will cause the edge to chip, but many musicians use it because of the permanence of the facing.

We can fine-tune rugged metal mouthpieces to a high degree, using small dimensions because metals do not need any least thickness measure to have strength. It proves terrific for baritone and tenor players with a small mouth or who want a smaller mouthpiece.

Plastic is common because it is a suitable material. Since the quality of production improved, it no longer cracks like it used to and it has high strength and permanence, making it the preferred choice for student's instruments because of the low cost.

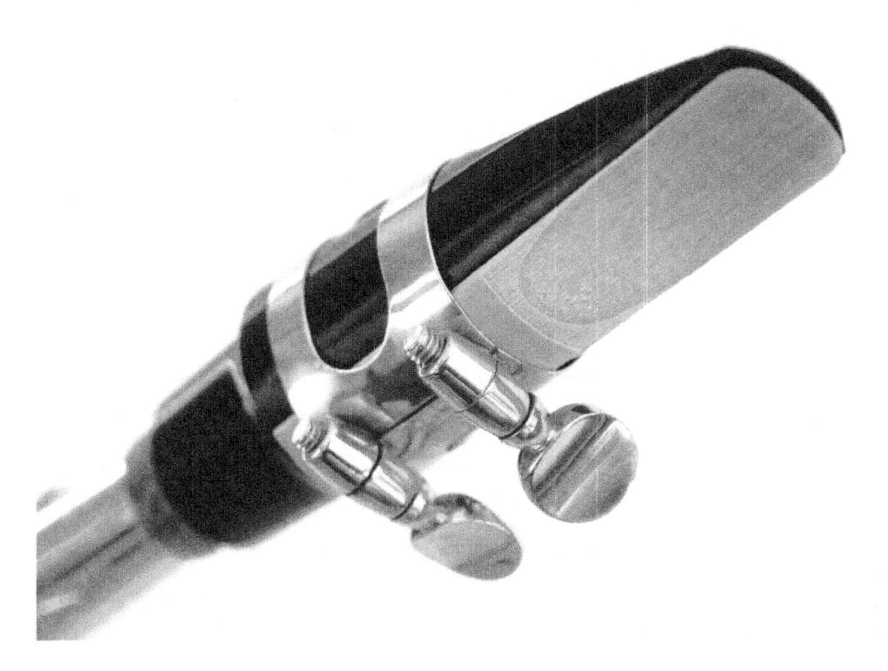

The ebonite or rod rubber mouthpiece is also a favorite. We can reface and tool the piece with ease, and it will not crack. It is permanent for holding a facing if you use it well. You must handle it with care because you will injure the facing or tip if you bump or drop it.

You must wipe the mouthpiece dry with a soft cloth both on the outside and inside. You can use lukewarm water and soap, but never boiling water. The narrow rails offer only slight resistance, so it remains difficult to control. It is wonderful if you want a rough projection and sometimes preferred by those who wish to produce this kind of sound, risking a squeak. Only experienced players must attempt this maneuver.

- **The Chamber**: Here, the tone gets its primary resonance. Though the facing is important, one has to consider that a magnificent chamber will produce a great tone irrespective of the type of facing you have. Even when it is a small mouthpiece, it will produce a great volume when it leads straight to the chamber. Also, it will have a greater edge than a large chamber that is not. Where there are straight sidewalls, there is room for more partials, whereas curved sidewalls make the sound more mellow. It is not possible to make generalizations because there are so many shapes in the sidewalls.

- **Mouthpiece Selection**: The selection of the mouthpiece is a lengthy and difficult process. One will do well to start with a standard or medium type mouthpiece. When your skill with the instrument improves, taste and style will take definite paths. One must take care to learn the right thing because you will have to repeat any mistake you commit until you rectify it. Bad habits cause an improper procedure along with a long and costly rectification process. For instance, if you choose a radical mouthpiece, it will set you far back on your path towards mastering the instrument. If you take the case of a person who opts for a mouthpiece with a long, open facing, he will have to bite to get the upper notes. His jaw will drop considerably while producing lower tones. If he allows this habit to develop, it will take years to correct it, even after he has taken the right position in his playing. Any experienced teacher will tell you this. It is not unusual to come across this sort of situation, and it is the self-taught student who remains prone to bad habits. We can rectify a few of these habits through the use of a moderate type of mouthpiece.

- **Note**: We can reface a mouthpiece, but it will not change the quality of the tone to any significant degree. Playing becomes easy for the student when he has a psychological advantage. The tone depends on the baffle and the mouthpiece chamber. When you do the refacing, include the baffle and the tip rail.

- **Improve the Tone**: If you use a rubber pad on top of the mouthpiece, it eases the vibration through the teeth. These vibrations can annoy some players. This rubber pad opens the mouth more so that the sound becomes mellower.

When the mouthpiece is set too high, cut it down with care using a fine file and have it re-polished. You must take care not to go through all the way. It's best to use the services of a professional to do this.

All saxophonists have had the dream that manufacturers will come up with a standardized system for marking the facing so that they convey meaning to the uninitiated. Even if this were only approximate, it would avoid a lot of confusion. Right now, there is no way to understand what all the hieroglyphics relating to tip openings and facings mean.

When you compare two mouthpieces, tune each of them separately. When mouthpieces are longer than normal, they need a separate cork placement.

The entire saxophone family has the same basic principle for mouthpiece construction. Because there is a difference in the mouthpiece's size, you need not always use the same facing. Each mouthpiece has its limitations. If one uses a poor embouchure or does not give enough air support, the mouthpiece cannot compensate.

Regular cleaning with water is important because germs accumulate inside the mouthpiece. You can get many diseases from this breeding ground. Also, calcified sediment gets deposited on the insides of the instrument, forming an invisible layer impossible to remove if you let it accumulate.

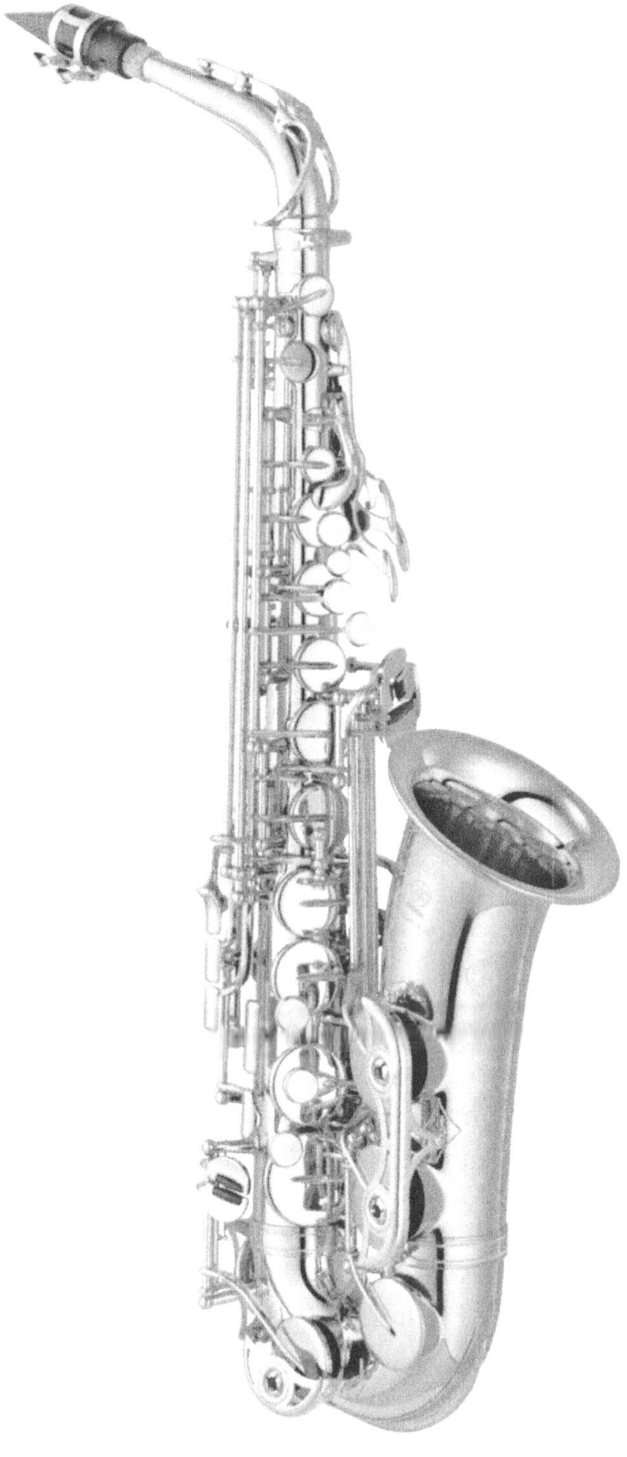

CHAPTER 7

SAXOPHONES FOR BEGINNERS

Alto saxophones have enriched the culture for centuries, especially in America, where one could hear the smooth, mellifluous sound from the street corner musician, hoping to get a bite to eat during the Great Depression. The best saxophonists have performed in top jazz clubs, adding its tone to the repertoire of delightful music. It became an instrument everyone revered, whatever genre they used it in.

LIST OF BEGINNER'S SAXOPHONES

For the beginner, the alto saxophone is the best one there is. He or she can express one's talent in full. Here are the best student alto saxophones and the review about them.

1. Yamaha YAS-280   Pick for Students in High School

2. Mendini by Cecilio MAS-L   Alto Saxophone Cheap and Best

3. Conn-Selmer AS711   Best Durable Beginners Saxophone

4. Jean-Paul AS-400   Top Saxophone for Serious Practice

5. Kaizer ASAX-1000LQ   A Terrific Saxophone for Young Students

6. Jupiter JAS1100SG   The Saxophone for Advanced Students

7. Yamaha YAS-480   Best Intermediate Budget Alto Sax

8. Selmer SAS280 La Voix II   Alto Sax with Great Looks

9. Yamaha YAS-26   Best Value Saxophone

10. Etude EAS-100   Helpful Beginners Saxophone

Yamaha YAS-280→Best for High School Students

Though it is on the pricier side, we recommend it for high school students. You get the rich Yamaha sounds, and with a little practice, you can create dream sounds. The alto saxophone has a sturdy build, which is good because it will take a while for the student to reach a professional level of playing. An intermediate saxophone will become unnecessary if you opt for the YAS-280 as it also suits band practice and playing small gigs. The good things about this instrument are:

- The material quality is excellent, so you remain protected against normal wear.
- The saxophone's action is wonderful, so it relieves the pressure acting on the student's hands and fingernails.
- Its clean and shiny finish makes it ready for the stage at all times.
- You get a neck strap and cleaning kit.
- All accessories needed to play this instrument are available and affordable.
- It has a wonderful sound, the same as an instrument, six times as costly.

The downside of this instrument is that the tabs can prove finicky when the testing is not proper. It is the best student alto saxophone; you will get professional quality sounds from the word go.

Mendini by Cecilio MAS-L→Alto Saxophone and the Most Cost Efficient

Here we have an instrument for the beginner that is pocket-friendly and helps the student with its friendly action. You get everything you need in the kit so you can start off immediately.

- The saxophone is easy to tune, and it keeps its tuning for a long time.
- You get an excellent sound quality.
- Because of its low price, it is a favorite with newbies. It is a best seller because of this.
- With the kit, you get a mouthpiece, neck strap, a hard case where you can put everything, gloves, a cleaning kit, a tuner, and reeds.
- When it is time to upgrade, you get a good resale value.
- Because of the exceptional quality of the materials used to make this instrument, it has terrific durability.

The inlays are fake mother-of-pearl, but you get a huge reduction in price. A tone booster is fitted with the instrument, but most people still find the sound a little rich. But considering it is a beginner's sax, this point will pass. The material, though good enough, is not comparable to that of more expensive instruments.

This is a wonderful beginner's saxophone for one who will make it to the big stage in due course. It is budget-friendly and, sure enough, the student will outgrow it. It gives you time to save for the costlier instrument you will buy.

Conn-Selmer AS711→Best Durable Beginner Saxophone

This Prelude student model is well-suited for the beginner saxophone player. It has a yellow brass finish on its body with clear lacquer. It helps students position their fingers properly and comfortably. They can develop accurate fingering techniques with ease. The A711 is lightweight at 3 pounds and combines performance with value.

- The kit includes ligature, cap, mouthpiece, and a case.
- The beginner and student will find this an affordable option.
- It has a ribbed construction with a detachable body. The body-to-body connection comes reinforced for stability and strength.
- You get rocking table keys, high F#, and articulated C#.
- Anyone can play it easily.
- It is durable.

You do not have a uniform note on all registers. It has a basic mouthpiece, so it will be a good idea to upgrade to a better one. This brand is trustworthy, and we know them to be producers of high-quality student's saxophones. There are a few who complain of delayed shipment from China and of air leaks. But you get a good price and quality.

Jean-Paul AS-400→Top Saxophone for Serious Players

Playing this instrument is difficult because it is an intermediate alto saxophone. It also costs more, so do not choose this instrument unless you are serious about learning the instrument. You do not want to waste money and effort needlessly.

Once you have learned to play, the instrument will help you play smooth jazz numbers with ease.

- Tone and sound are superb and comparable to the other saxophones, much costlier than this one.

- It offers two finishes: a silver lacquer finish and the standard brass finish with lacquer.

- Because of the smooth action, there is a lot of relief for the hands. You can play the instrument for hours on end effortlessly.

- Tuning this saxophone is easy, and the tuning remains for a long time. You will not have to keep tuning the instrument when you practice solos or are jamming with the band.

- It has a lovely note arrangement that allows the user to take on many notes within a short time. This is useful for all styles, but especially while playing classical music.

This is a terrific saxophone for a beginner and even an intermediate player, whatever genre he is playing. It does not cost too much, which helps those who are on a budget. This company has gone to great lengths to provide a quality instrument that rivals professional level instruments. You also get top-notch customer service. If you face any problem, they make sure you get the replacement parts in time so you will not miss a single session of practice.

Kaizer ASAX-1000LQ→A Terrific Saxophone for Young Students

Here is the best cheap alto saxophone available on the market now. Kaizer ASAX-1000LQ is also the best saxophone under $500. Spending thousands of dollars on an instrument is not realistic for a beginner. These budget-friendly saxophones help the student become familiar with the world Adolphe Sax invented through his instrument.

- The sax comes with a case shaped perfectly to provide perfect protection while storing and moving it. You get a ligature set with a mouthpiece. And there is a cleaning kit along with gloves to help you maintain the instrument.

- When you buy this sax, you get a long list of accessories to enhance the user's experience.

- It has a fast action, great product intonation control through the pro pads, and significant response. It helps the player reach professional standards in a short time.

- The solid brass body has great tonality, giving sound better than that of the average budget sax.

- You get a lifetime warranty that is valid even when you resell the instrument. The warranty stays with the instrument, not with the person.

- There is a refund guarantee from the company for 45 days, which is more than what most stores offer.

The downside is that many users have experienced air leaks at all points of the product. This leads to a broken saxophone, which means one has to use the lifetime warranty to get a replacement. Another common complaint is that the metal is too soft. The quality of the sound diminishes because of this.

This saxophone helps the student begin his foray into the world of music. He may stop playing after a while but beginning with a budget saxophone will help him learn how to play this wonderful instrument.

Jupiter JAS1100SG→The Saxophone for Advanced Students

For those wishing to transit from beginner to intermediate player, Jupiter JAS1100SG is the correct choice because it can produce the great tones you expect to play.

This instrument comes with a silver-plated Sona-Pure neck made with artisan tooling. Annealing creates a dark vintage tone. There is silver plating on the brass body, and the playability is excellent. The contoured table keys help the left-handed player, while you have improved agility and comfort through the tilting Bb rocker arm.

- The body and neck have sophistication and style.
- It has a wonderful vintage jazz zone.
- You also get a wood-framed case for artists' series included.
- It is possible to adjust the lower and upper stacks.
- Special keys include front F, high F#, and tilting G# to Bb table keys.
- The fingering is comfortable.
- You get enhanced playability.

Because of its high cost (more than $2,000), it might not be possible for an average player to get this instrument.

Jupiter is one of the oldest instrument makers and one of the instrument's biggest distributors for all schools in the world. Their specialty is woodwind instruments made for easy playability, durability, and reliability.

For the semi-professional and advanced players, Jupiter makes the intermediate Eb alto saxophone.

Yamaha YAS-480→Best Intermediate Budget Alto Sax

The Yamaha YAS-480 is a versatile, intermediate alto saxophone made for high school students. It helps him play in the school band or in a symphony or start his band with his friends.

It has a high-end Yamaha design that features a fast response along with highly accurate intonation. The 62-style professional neck helps it carry a more mature sound. Musicians might sometimes use Custom EX or Custom Z Yamaha necks.

- High intonation accuracy.
- It is silver-plated.
- The low B-C# mechanism remains corrected from the previous models.
- You get increased playability and comfort from the left-hand seesaw keys.
- It has separate guards for keys and screw cap stoppers we can adjust.
- You get the included 62-style neck.
- The bell has a hand-engraved pattern.
- It has a warm tone.
- The response is quick.

The downside is its case is soft padded instead of a hard case. But if one prefers the soft case, this will prove a blessing. Also, it is pricey for those who are still in school.

If one is serious about playing the instrument and wants an upgrade, then Yamaha YAS-480 is the best option. It will see you well into the professional playing level.

One should not get put off by the price as the sax is durable and will last you a long time. Yamaha also gives warranties.

Selmer SAS280 La Voix II→Alto Sax with Great Looks

If you look to draw attention to your sax playing, then the Selmer SAS280 La Voix II alto saxophone is the way to go. This is an intermediate instrument with black nickel plating that helps improve its looks compared to traditional silver or brass-plated instruments.

The key work is fluid in this saxophone with perfect intonation and its bell is traditional-sized. The SAS280 gives you a focused tone and blended sound.

- It has perfect intonation.
- Its terrific looks will make you the center of attraction in your band.
- You get the ligature, cap, and mouthpiece along with the instrument.
- The sound is consistent from the low end up to altissimo.
- There is professional styling of the keys to help make fingering accurate.
- The keys show great fluidity.

The negative point about this instrument is you might experience a wild tone when you switch registers. But with experience, it becomes possible to control this.

There aren't too many negative points about the Selmer SAS280 La Voix II. This is because Selmer has a reputation for making high-quality instruments.

When a student is ready to step up to one that has professional-level sound quality, he can choose this amazing alto saxophone. It also suits the semi-pro user who wants a cheap professional-sounding instrument.

Yamaha YAS-26→Best Value Saxophone

One of the top choices for a beginner who plans to play saxophone for a long time is Yamaha YAS-26. It is not the cheapest one around but is a significant investment for one who wants a long musical career.

This entry-level saxophone combines the design used in professional Yamaha saxophones with state-of-the-art production techniques. This makes the instrument give a fast and accurate response and tone. Among the fresh features included in this instrument, the top ones are the redesigned neck receiver, improved B-C# connection, and a thumb rest that is adjustable. The new design of the neck receiver makes playing easy.

- Thumb rest is adjustable.
- Better, more durable screws in the neck designer in the new design.
- Outstanding durability.
- Improvement in the B-C# connection.
- Nickel-plated keys.
- You get a case along with the instrument.
- There is a mouthpiece, neck, and strap included in the kit.
- It is light at 11.68 pounds.

This is a student beginner model and will not suit the more advanced players.

The Yamaha YAS-26 is an excellent instrument, a step above the low-end saxophone in the budget range.

While you may want to spend something more on your entry-level saxophone, this instrument is a good intermediate instrument that gives you value for money. In the long term, the Yamaha quality gives you the best return for your investment.

Etude EAS-100→Helpful Beginner Saxophone

This instrument is for students. The Etude EAS-100 has wonderful tone production and has all the accessories a beginner will need to play the instrument. This includes ligature, care products, mouthpiece, and a case.

You can take the EAS-100 from the case and start playing it because they have already set it up. The cost of a brand new one of these instruments is only a couple of hundred dollars. It is a durable and affordable instrument.

- It comes ready to play.
- The tone of the instrument is excellent.
- Weight of the instrument is light at 10 pounds.
- This instrument is long-lasting.
- It has a brightly colored lacquer finish.
- All the extras you need, such as the reeds, case, and neck strap, remain included.

The shortcoming is the neck strap is short. Also, you will want to upgrade to a different mouthpiece and better reeds.

This student alto sax has the best value for students who pick up the instrument for the first time. It has a durable construction, and with less than $500, students can make it last forever.

What are the Best Alto Saxophones Brands?

An alto saxophone uses the vibration of the wind to produce sound. Hence, we call it a woodwind instrument. The most common saxophone to play is the alto sax, with two others coming behind it. The smaller one is the soprano saxophone, and the one larger is the tenor saxophone.

For all the saxophones, the fingering positions are the same. This allows you to play any sax with ease, and you will not have to learn any extra notes. The only thing that will change is the size and sound of each instrument.

New students can pick an instrument from one of the five brands. They offer professional quality, which means upgrading will not be a problem. Here is the list of the best saxophones for beginners:

1. Conn-Selmer

One of the best things about jazz music is the merger between Selmer and Conn. The Conn brand dates way back to the 1900s. Jazz legends such as Paul Desmond and John Coltrane belong to the Selmer club.

The new Conn-Selmer company makes saxophones in all ranges. People respect them for their quality of tone, longevity, and sound. And all are handmade professional instruments.

2. Yamaha

Most school students would have heard of Yamaha, as it is the most popular brand in any music shop or school.

Yamaha has a long record of making high-quality student musical instruments at a great price. It is the best brand of alto saxophone for students and kids interested in the alto saxophone.

3. Mendini by Cecilio

For those looking for cheap alto sax (sax on a budget), go for the Mendini by Cecilio. You may get them from Amazon, so buying is not a problem. The construction of these instruments is decent, and the price is the lowest in the group.

4. Yanagisawa

This brand began at the end of the 1900s as a brass wind company. Yanagisawa produces professional-grade saxophones.

The instruments produced by this brand have a warmer tone compared to those produced by other companies in the market. The tone is more resonant and pitch true. They do not produce student models, but you can buy an intermediate level instrument if you are serious about learning music.

5. Jupiter

The rise of Jupiter in the musical world was phenomenal. Since they were established in the 1930s, they built a full line of instruments and made them available to individual musicians and school children.

Jupiter has a reputation for its superior instruments at all levels, including the student level. Their plant is company-owned, so they make all the individual parts, and they outsource nothing. This ensures consistent quality of the instruments.

Best Intermediate Saxophones

Alto Saxophones

Yamaha YAS-480 Intermediate Eb Alto Saxophone

Yamaha instruments have a reputation for their perfection, though the price is comparatively higher than other brands. But you can find an affordable one, and at this intermediate-level, you can also pick one alto saxophone you can afford, like the YAS-480.

Features: The YAS-480 weighs in at 18.9 pounds. The instrument is silver-plated and has a hand-engraved bell with a professional-quality 62-style neck. This helps you produce a warm and mature sound.

This instrument comes with a redesigned system of the octave key. It helps improve the response of the system. To improve and make the playability easy, it has left-hand seesaw keys.

Budget-Friendly or Not: This instrument is medium-priced. You get wonderful features and improved playability and quality accessories with the kit, making it worth investing in.

Accessories Included: There is a whole range of accessories included with this instrument. For one, you get the reeds, so you will not have to shell out money for that. You also get a case and cleaning swabs to help you clean and maintain the instrument. The alto sax mouthpiece you get is of high quality.

The plus points of this instrument are you get a lot of accessories. The left-hand seesaw keys help playability. And the bell comes hand engraved.

Jupiter Intermediate Eb Alto Saxophone

For beginners who have already begun playing the saxophone, this intermediate alto saxophone is a wise choice because it will develop you into a more mature player. For the professional level musician, it serves as an instrument for practice. The Jupiter Eb Alto saxophone comes in two colors - gold lacquered and silver-plated.

Features: This sax is heavy at 25 pounds. It has a hand-engraved bell and screws to adjust the lower and upper stacks. You see a blue steel spring in the key of Eb that adds to the instrument's durability and strength.

Budget-Friendly or Not: This is going to cost you money, so if you want a budget sax, look somewhere else. If you want to get this instrument, you might need to save up for it first. If you buy it, you will have the happiness of playing a superior instrument.

Accessories Included: The Jupiter Intermediate Eb Alto saxophone owners get the exquisite Artist Series case of durable and lightweight wood frame and there is a mouthpiece to help with the intonations. The accessories are available everywhere, so if you need anything, you can order and get it. You get a five-year warranty with this instrument.

The plus points of this instrument are the hand-engraved bell and the included accessories. You have the key of Eb, and the sax is heavy.

TENOR SAXOPHONES

Allora Vienna Series Intermediate Tenor Saxophone AATS-501

This best tenor sax is lacquer with a ribbed construction and has lots of improved and great features. Any kind of saxophonist can play this instrument. Beginners will be happy to know more about this intermediate saxophone. The professional saxophone player will be happy to know about the similarity this has with professional level saxophones.

Features: The dimensions of this tenor sax are 31.5x12.5x8.5 inches, and it weighs 17.35 pounds. It has professionally styled keys, so professional players feel at home with this instrument. It helps intermediate players become professional level players.

Budget-Friendly or Not: Allora Vienna series intermediate saxophones are expensive. It looks beautiful because they make it out of quality material. You get plenty of accessories with this instrument. The high price is because it has some features that resemble those of professional level saxophones.

Accessories Included: The Allora gig-bag comes with the instrument. The back strap helps you carry the instrument with ease. Also, you get the cap and ligature, and an intermediate level mouthpiece is present. You can easily replace it with something you like. To care for this instrument, you need the Allora care products.

To sum up, this tenor sax comes with accessories. The exceptional quality of the material ensures the high quality of this instrument. It has professionally styled keys. And there are many advanced features.

Yamaha YTS-480 Intermediate Bb Tenor Saxophone

The Yamaha YTS-480 produces a powerful sound with great warmth. It is one of the best intermediate tenor saxophones available. It is durable because of the yellow brass used to make this instrument. It has polyester key buttons. This tenor sax has drawn tone holes and waterproof leather pads.

Features: This Yamaha tenor saxophone has the dimensions 34.4x10.8x17.1 inches and weighs 24.2 pounds. You see a quick response with the YTS-480 in the key of b-flat. It is a durable instrument because it has high-quality parts, but many users replace the neck to improve playability. The instrument is hand engraved. In short, it has outstanding features and Yamaha durability.

Budget-Friendly or Not: It is not budget-friendly. It has many features that make it a worthwhile investment, and users who bought it are not sorry they did. There are many alternative cheaper intermediate brands of saxophones available.

Accessories Included: With this offer, you get the professional Yamaha case. It is a semi-hard backpack that makes carrying your sax a breeze. They give you a five-year manufacturer's warranty with this saxophone.

To sum up, you get a durable quality instrument. You also get a professional case from Yamaha. The instrument is hand-engraved, and you can replace the neck.

SOPRANO SAXOPHONES

Allora Vienna Series Curved Soprano Saxophone AASC-503

This is an outstanding model with solid construction and terrific looks. The lacquered brass body, keys, bell, and neck give it a stunning appearance. Beginners can use it, but this instrument will suit any level player. It produces a magnificent sound.

Features: The instrument has Bb as its key. Its bow and bell are hand engraved. The dimensions of this soprano sax are 20x11.3x7.9 inches.

The instrument is light at 9.5 pounds. It has a smooth and light action that helps even novices play the instrument fluently. It has rapid movement from low intonation to high with a smooth action.

Budget-Friendly or Not: This intermediate-level sax would suit a beginner because it helps the action. This helps the student learn fast. The price is low for the number of features it has.

Accessories Included: The Allora Vienna series AASC-503 has a case strong enough to protect the instrument from damage. You get back straps so you can carry this case on your back. The mouthpiece helps you make beautiful sounds, while the care products help you protect the instrument and maintain it. The sax is durable and long-lasting. Ligature and cap are present in the kit.

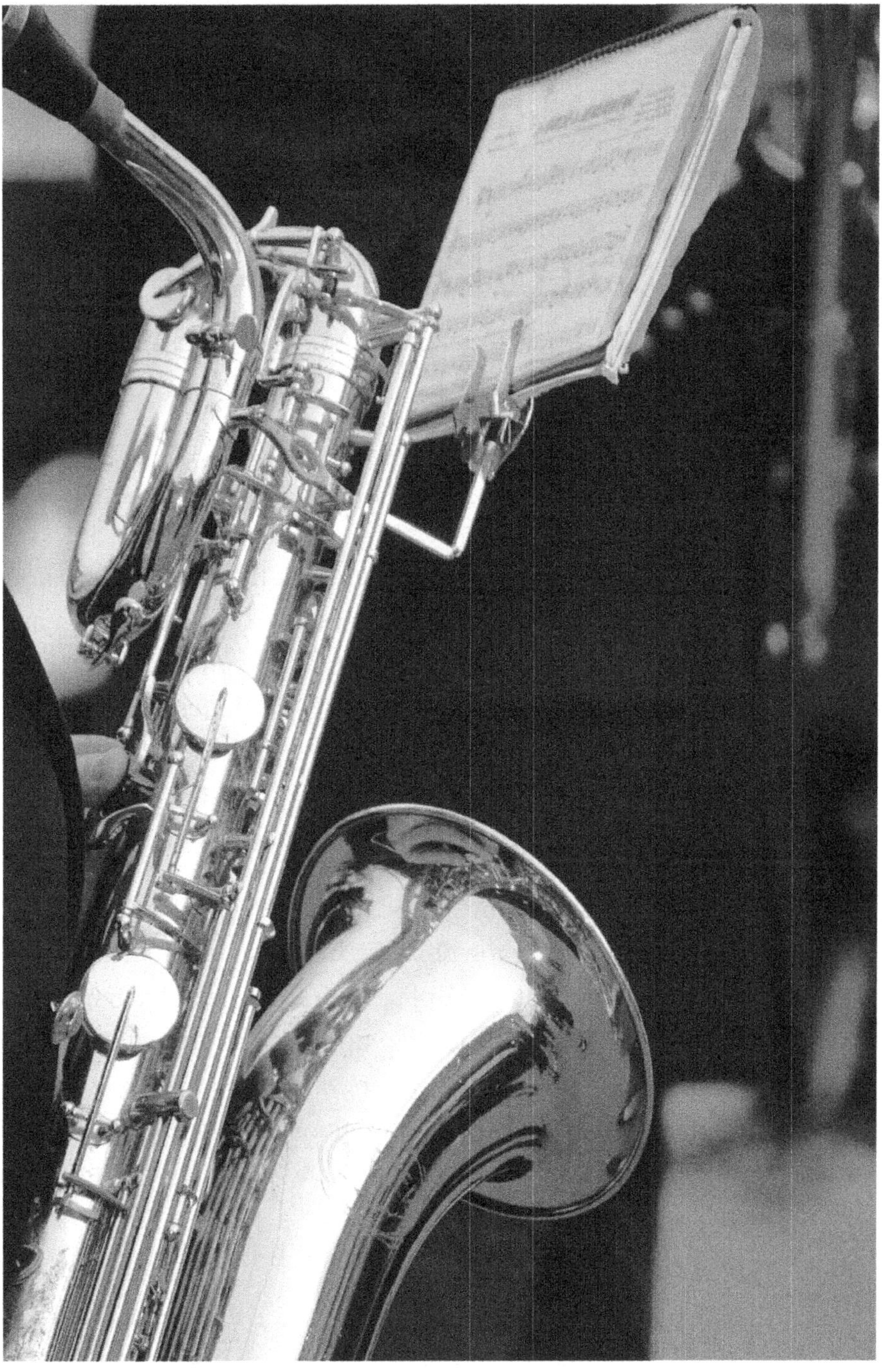

CHAPTER 8

MAJOR SCALES ON THE SAXOPHONE

All the major scales have the same structure, with the first note being the root note. This is followed by two whole steps and one half-step. After this, take three whole steps and one half-step. If we denote the whole step by T and a half-step by S, the pattern is TTSTTTS. Say we need the C major scale, we begin with the C. After this, we need two whole steps - D and E. The next note is a half-step S given by F. Now take three whole steps, GAB. Finish with one half-step, C.

Why is this right? We get the musical scale AA#BCC#DD#EFF#GG#A according to music theory. If you observe, we represent all the notes on the musical instrument using the alphabets from A to G. Each note has a sharp note meaning it is one half-step up from the original. So, from A, we have one half-step to get A#, after which the next note is B. In this way, we can go up to G. Here, we take a half-step G# and then complete the octave by playing A. This A note is higher in pitch than the original A at the place where you started.

READ MUSIC

The way to read music is to understand the names of the notations and symbols first.

Here they are:

The Clef Symbols

By the staff lines, we mean the set of five lines and four spaces used to write notes. The notes are circles full, shaded as black or small. We look at the size of the circle that tells us how much time we give to it. The figure on the left extreme is the G clef, denoting the notes in the upper region of the piano. As we go right, we see the A note and then further right another note A. This second A is one octave higher up. The next symbol we see is the F clef, denoting the notes of the lower part of the piano. We also call the G clef the treble clef, while the F clef is the bass clef. As a point of interest, the line written above the staff lines is called the ledger line. When needed, we use it to write notes that go way above (or way below) the normal range.

Staff Notation

The treble clef lines represent the notes - EGBDF, while the spaces are FACE reading the notes from the bottom upwards. You see that the first line at the bottom is E and the next space is F, which is the next note on the musical scale. The notes of the bass clef are GBDFA, and the spaces are ACEG.

Between the upper and lower staff, we have the middle C. This is the C occurring in the fourth octave of the piano. It serves as the basis for tuning all musical instruments.

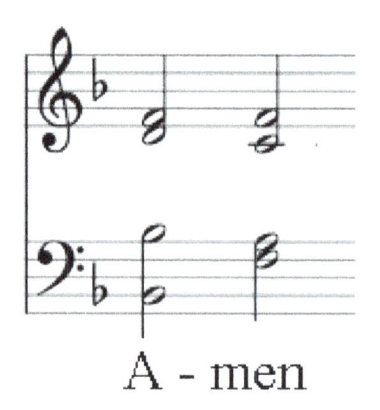

A - men

Here we can read the middle C as the note on the small line drawn below the staff lines with the treble clef on top.

The B note is flat, meaning the scale is F major and you will read more about this in the section called Circle of Fifths. To sing Amen, we use four notes for A and four more for men. The four notes are (from the bottom to the top) B B D F and F A C F. See if you can make it out.

THE SHARP AND FLAT NOTATION

Here is the symbol for sharp. And you can see the b symbol given in the passage above denoting flat. The sharp symbol means the note remains raised by one half-note, while the flat symbol shows it gets dropped by one half-note. So, Fb (F flat) means the note drops to E. B# (B sharp) means the note gets raised by one half-note so that it becomes C. Remember the sequence of notes in the musical scale is CC#DD#EFF#GG#AA#BC. There is no sharp note for either B or E.

While all the notes have a sharp as FF#GG# and so on, when we come to B, it goes straight to C, and when we come to E, it goes straight to F.

We can use either sharp or flat notation to write music. So, instead of writing G#, we can write Ab. Or, instead of writing Eb, we can write D#. The twelve semitones make up the musical scale. The starting note is the root note meaning that if we start from C (and go to the next octave C), the root note is C.

THE MAJOR AND MINOR SCALE

When we begin with C, we see the pattern Tone Tone Semitone and then Tone Tone Tone Semitone. Tone represents one whole step comprising two semitones. Start from C and apply the pattern interval. C + one whole tone = D. D + one whole tone = E. We have used two whole steps. Now, we need a semitone. One semitone takes us to F (here, we don't have any sharp note) from E. After this, we need three whole steps. F + one whole tone = G. G + one whole tone = A. A + one whole tone = B. Now, we need one semitone, and that will take us to C. This is the octave note that is higher in pitch but keeps the same tone. This is the major scale pattern.

The key signature (set of sharp symbols) shows this to be A major scale. Discounting the first note G, the root note is in the second space and we go up seven notes to reach the octave note A.

The Minor Scale

The minor scale has three variations. First, we have the natural minor followed by the melodic minor and the harmonic minor. These scales differ in the way we choose the notes. Other than that, they all have a sad note in them while on the major scale, the notes give the feeling of happiness. In the melodic minor, the notes change when we ascend and descend the scale. It means we use one set of notes to climb up the octave and use another set to descend.

A Natural Minor Scale

We see the notes of the A natural minor are ABCDEFGA. There are no sharp notes in this scale. It resembles the C major scale in this respect because they have a relationship with each other.

A Harmonic Minor Scale

In the ascending and descending scale, A harmonic minor has the same set of notes. It differs from the natural minor in its seventh note which remains raised one half-step. So, we get G# instead of G.

A Melodic Minor Scale

In the melodic minor, the notes will change when we go up and down. In the first figure, we see the notes of the ascending scale.

In the second, there are the notes of the descending scale, which are all-natural notes. The sixth and seventh notes are sharp in the ascending scale and remain raised by one semitone. So, we have F# and G# instead of F and G.

To sum up, the harmonic minor scale is almost the same as the natural scale but has a raised seventh degree. In the melodic minor scale, the sixth and seventh degrees remain raised for the ascending part and lower to their natural minor state when descending.

Music Theory

To understand how music works, you must read the music theory. You might find it intimidating at first, but musical development begins with a proper understanding of how it works. When you understand the theory, you can explain how the phenomena in musical compositions sounded. You have got the basic start by developing the sound. The sound is the first thing the listeners notice when you play. Even when you play a lot of scales and fancy combinations of notes, it will not have any effect unless you have the sound.

Make the Sound

The basics of sound are these:

- Melody
- Rhythm
- Harmony

Melody

Melody is important but hard to achieve but with practice you will be able to write and sing melodies. A melody is a linear sequence of notes that the listener hears as one single entity and is the foreground to the backing elements, such as the combination of pitch and rhythm.

When you sing Happy Birthday, you sing a melody. We produce melodies through the human voice and using instruments such as the guitar or the saxophone. A melody transforms into harmony when you play many sequences of notes at the same time. This is how we make chords.

Many factors affect the sound, from embouchure to the air stream and more. It is important to play the sax a lot because you will develop a rapport with the sound. You will get to know what to do to make the sax sound sweet or loud. Playing daily helps you develop control by exercising the muscles of your face so make sure you play at least 15 minutes each day.

You have instrumental melodies and vocal melodies. Depending on the genre of the music you play, one of them will dominate the other. For instance, you will have a lot of instrumental melodies in jazz music, whereas vocal melodies will be more in pop music. Having a good mouthpiece and ligature is important to get an agreeable sound from your sax.

Pentatonic Scale

The pentatonic scale is the foundation for almost all music we play. It has five notes (Penta) and includes the major and minor forms. One way to construct the pentatonic scale is to start from the root on the Circle of Fifths and take five consecutive notes. So, what is the circle of fifths?

MAJOR SCALES ON THE SAXOPHONE

The musical scale has 12 chromatic pitches. Chromatic is another way to refer to the side-by-side arrangement of notes. Each note remains distanced from the next by a semitone. When we play all the notes one after the other, we get the chromatic scale. This scale is useful for beginners to help them become familiar with their instrument and with the sound.

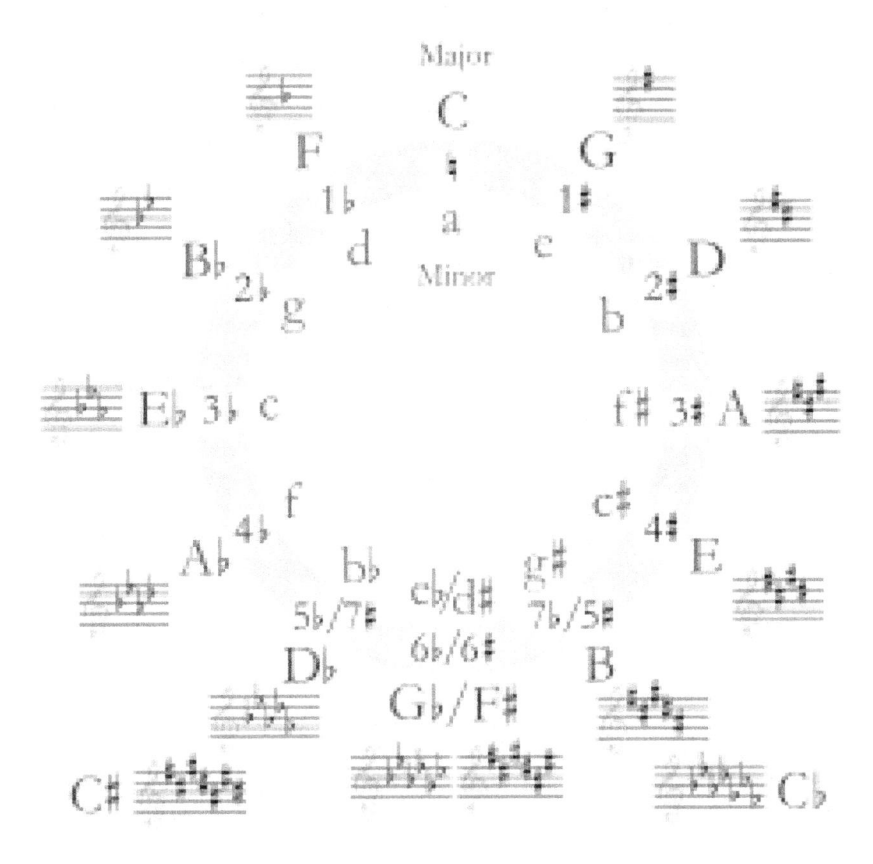

Major

C
F — G
1♭ — 1♯
a
B♭ 2♭ — d — e — 2♯ D
g — Minor — b
E♭ 3♭ c — f♯ 3♯ A
f — c♯
A♭ 4♭ — 4♯ E
b♭ — g♯
5♭/7♯ — c♭/d♯ — 7♭/5♯
D♭ — 6♭/6♯ — B
G♭/F♯
C♯ — C♭

Using the Circle of Fifths, we arrange the chromatic scale as a sequence of fifths.

When we use the root note C, the consecutive notes are G, D, A, and E. So, the pentatonic scale is the root, major second, major third, perfect fifth, and major sixth. It is CDEGAC.

Solfege is a framework for the melodies. We can also refer to it as solfeggio or solfa. It helps you understand the architecture behind the music. In this, we assign one syllable to each pitch of the musical scale. So, the notes of each scale, major, minor, seventh, and so on, have a different syllable. For the major scale, these syllables are do re mi fa sol la ti do. It is easy to sing the syllables instead of the letters A, B, and so on. When we compare the pentatonic and major scales, we see that we get the pentatonic scale when we omit fa and ti from the major scale.

MEMORIZE THE PENTATONIC SCALE

do   re   mi   fa   so   la   ti   do

In the Aiken shape system, we denote the notes of the musical scale like this:

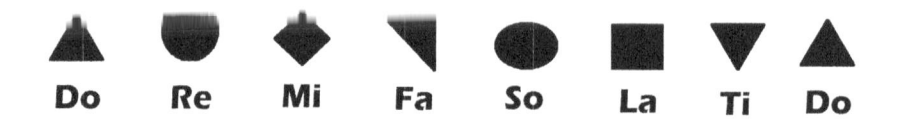

Do   Re   Mi   Fa   So   La   Ti   Do

What you need to concentrate on is the placement of the notes. C is the middle C, one line below the staff lines. The next note is D below the staff lines. The first line of the staff is E, and the first space is F. And it goes on until the octave note C. Here you learn that there are two kinds of solfege systems - the fixed Do and the movable Do systems. In the fixed Do system, the first Do is always C. So, re will be D and so on. In the movable Do system, the first Do can be any root note. The scale pattern will follow the notes according to the root. If we use E as the root note, then do re mi fa sol la ti do will be EF#G#ABC#D#E (Check the Circle of Fifths for the key signature - E major will have four sharps in its key signature). If we change it to G, then the notes become GABCDEF#G (only one sharp in the key signature).

Understand Solfege

Solfege will help you recognize the interval patterns in a song and identify the scale. The musical concepts of the pentatonic scale have their basis on folk and traditional music which helped in the evolution of the music genres such as rock and modern blues because it forms a fantastic improvisational framework. The advantages of using this pentatonic scale are:

- Because its notes are all consonants, it fits well with all kinds of music. You can use any backing track for this scale.
- It is easy to memorize the patterns for the keyboard and transpose them to any key.
- You can play them over various modes with ease. These are modes such as the Mixolydian, Ionian, and Lydian.

The pentatonic system goes well with the CAGED system for the guitar. The CAGED system is a set of five fingering patterns we can use across the guitar's fretboard. You can unlock the power of the guitar using these patterns. For the sax player, it will help to know the way the guitarist plays, so you find it easy to make the changes when you play along with him during a performance.

Solfege is an aural, a musical language that helps you write what you hear.

SOLFEGE FOR THE MINOR SCALE

The first thing to notice is that the third degree will remain one semitone lower in the minor scale than the major scale. The scale's name will depend on the starting note, which will also be the ending note. You include any accidentals associated with the scale.

Note: The accidentals are the notes that are not natural notes. It refers to the sharp (or flat) notes that are part of the scale. You can see the number of accidentals the scale will have by referring to the key signature in the Circle of Fifths. The natural minor form will have the pattern TSTTSTT, where T represents a whole note (two semitones), and S is a semitone.

Harmonic Minor

For the harmonic minor, the pattern is TSTTS(3T)S. The melodic minor has two patterns. The ascending scale pattern is TSTTTTS, while the descending pattern is TTSTTST. Please note that the scale degree in both the major and minor is the same. This refers to the note in the scale counting from the root note. The fourth degree of the C major scale is F because it is the fourth note in the C scale (CDEF). We see major and minor keys have two kinds of relationships - relative a relative one and a parallel one. The syllables for the natural minor scale are do re me fa sol le te do. Note the change in the third, sixth, and seventh syllables.

In the harmonic minor scale, the seventh remains raised so that the seventh syllable becomes ti instead of te. The scale is do re me fa sol le ti do. In the melodic minor scale, one more note gets changed. This is the sixth note le that becomes la as in the major scale. The entire note sequence is do re me fa sol la ti do. The descending melodic minor scale will have the pattern do te le sol fa me re do.

PARALLEL AND RELATIVE RELATIONSHIP

In the parallel relationship, the major key shares a tonic (Do) with the minor. You can see this in an example C major and C minor. They have the same tonic C. We say C minor is the parallel scale of C major.

In a relative relationship, the key signature is the same as another scale. For instance, C major has the key signature zero sharps. The relative scale is A minor. A minor also has no sharps in its key signature. C major and A minor have a relative relationship and the. key points of the relationship are:

- The tonic of the major scale is three and a half steps above that of the minor scale.
- Relative scales have the same key signature.

Enharmonic notes can show how relationships change when we choose another note. For instance, Db has a relative relationship with Bb. See the three-and-a-half steps - Db, D, Cb, Bb. But Db scale does not share a relative relationship with the A# scale even though A# and Bb are enharmonic. This is because Bb has 5 flats in its key signature. This is the same as that of Db, which also has 5 flats while A# minor has 7 sharps. Since this key signature is not the same as that of Db, A# and Bb do not share a relative relationship.

USE HARMONY IN MUSIC

Harmony plays the dominant role in music. Though we cannot do this by wishing for it, saxophonists with skill and an innovative spirit can make harmonious music.

Creative music is always interesting to listen to. We must play two or three notes at the same time to create harmony. The way the notes combine forms the basis for the harmony. Different genres of music have specific note combinations. Here is a look at some popular combinations:

Name of the Scale	Degrees	Note Interval
Acoustic scale	1 2 3 #4 5 6 b7	W-W-W-H-W-H-W
Aeolian mode (or natural minor scale)	1 2 b3 4 5 b6 b7	W-H-W-W-H-W-W
Altered scale (or Super Locrian scale)	1 b2 b3 b4 b5 b6 b7	H-W-H-W-W-W-W
Augmented scale	1 b3 3 5 #5 7	3H-H-3H-H-3H-H
Bebop dominant scale	1 2 3 4 5 6 b7 7	W-W-H-W-W-H-H-H
Blues scale	1 b3 4 b5 5 b7	3H-W-H-H-3H-W
Chromatic scale	1#1 2#2 3 4#4 5#5 6#6 7b7 6 b6 5b5 4 3b3 2b2 1	H-H-H-H-H-H-H-H-H-H-H
Dorian mode	1 2 b3 4 5 6 b7	W-H-W-W-W-H-W

Major Scales On The Saxophone

Flamenco mode	1 b2 3 4 5 b6 7	H-3H-H-W-H-3H-H
"Gypsy" scale	1 2 b3 #4 5 b6 b7	W-H-3H-H-H-W-W
Harmonic major scale	1 2 3 4 5 b6 7	W-W-H-W-H-3H-H
Harmonic minor scale	1 2 b3 4 5 b6 (♮)7	W-H-W-W-H-3H-H
Hungarian major scale	1 #2 3 #4 5 6 b7	3H-H-W-H-W-H-W
Ionian mode or major scale	1 2 3 4 5 6 7	W-W-H-W-W-W-H
Locrian mode	1 b2 b3 4 b5 b6 b7	H-W-W-H-W-W-W
Lydian mode	1 2 3 #4 5 6 7	W-W-W-H-W-W-H
Major bebop scale	1 2 3 4 5 (#5/b6) 6 7	W-W-H-W-(H-H)-W-H
Major Locrian scale	1 2 3 4 b5 b6 b7	W-W-H-H-W-W-W
Major pentatonic scale	1 2 3 5 6	W-W-3H-W-3H

Melodic minor scale	1 2♭3-4 5♮6♮7 8♭7♭6 5 4♭3 2 1	W-H-W-W-W-W-H (ascending) W-W-H-W-W-H-W (descending)
Melodic minor scale (ascending)	1 2 ♭3 4 5 6 7	W-H-W-W-W-W-H
Minor pentatonic scale	1 ♭3 4 5 ♭7	3H-W-W-3H-W
Mixolydian mode or Adonai malakh mode	1 2 3 4 5 6 ♭7	W-W-H-W-W-H-W
Persian scale	1 ♭2 3 4 ♭5 ♭6 7	H-3H-H-H-W-3H-H
Phrygian dominant scale	1 ♭2 3 4 5 ♭6 ♭7	H-3H-H-W-H-W-W
Phrygian mode	1 ♭2 ♭3 4 5 ♭6 ♭7	H-W-W-W-H-W-W
Whole tone scale	1 2 3 ♯4 ♯5 ♯6	W-W-W-W-W-W

Major Scales On The Saxophone

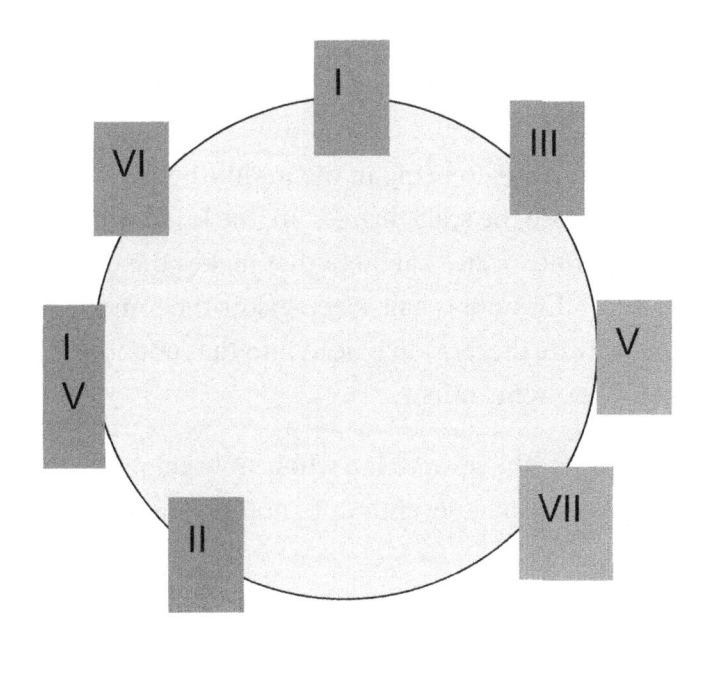

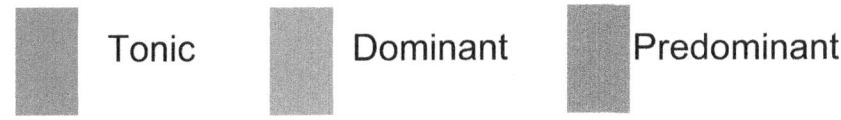

VI, I, III → Tonic   V, VII → Dominant   II, IV → Predominant

We use Roman numerals to represent the chords, each relating to the root note that we choose.

I   ii   iii   IV   V   vi   vii

C   D   E   F   G   A   B

C Major - D minor - E minor - F major - G major - A diminished - B minor

For tonal music, the main functional notes are tonic, predominant, and dominant. The first and last notes of the scale are tonic, the note above it is supertonic, and the one below is subtonic. We find the third degree is the Mediant, while the sixth is the submediant. Also, the subdominant is the same distance below the tonic as the dominant is above it.

The term Mediant refers to being in the middle between the tonic and the dominant. We see the scale degrees are the same, whether we refer to the major or minor scale. The note that makes the difference is the seventh degree. If this note is half a step below the tonic, it is a leading tone and it will create the tension to lead into the root note. This occurs in melodic and harmonic minor.

In the natural minor, the seventh is a whole note below the tonic where it becomes a subtonic. The seventh does not show a desire to lead into the tonic.

Rhythm in Music

Rhythm means stream or flow and is an essential ingredient in music. Music is a combination of sound and silence. Here we will see what the different rhythms are. Rhythm can exist without melody, but the melody cannot exist without rhythm. They string the rhythm together as smaller pieces like beads.

Beat

The smallest unit of rhythm is a beat, and it has a periodic repetition.

Tempo

When the music has a fast tempo, the beat is moving along at a quick pace. We also have slow tempo and moderate tempo music.

Rubato

Sometimes we need to slow the tempo of the music to bring more clarity or make it easy to play the instruments used to make the music. Tempo rubato - robbed time - exists in the framework of an inflexible beat.

Time

This refers to the way one plays the notes in a measure. The notes remain divided into groups of twos, threes, fours, or more groups to make the music pleasant to hear. You can read this at the beginning of the music score as the time signature. It has the form 2/4, 4/8, 2/2, and so on. The symbol 4/1 shows us there are 4 notes of one full note in each bar, 4/2 shows four half notes, and ⅜ shows there are three eighth notes to each bar.

Metre

In ancient Greece, where the origins of music occurred, poetry and classical music were parts of one single art form. So, there is an equivalence in the feet of classical poetry and music.

CHAPTER 9

BEGINNER SOPRANO SAXOPHONE TECHNIQUES

The Soprano saxophone is one of the most challenging and rewarding members of the saxophone family and it takes longer to master the intricacies compared to those of alto, baritone, or tenor saxophones. The soprano sax continues its reign as a popular solo voice in classical and jazz music, though they often use it in the saxophone quartet as an ensemble instrument.

INSTRUMENT SELECTION

It is as difficult to find a high-quality soprano as it is to find any other instrument to replace it. One reason is there are fewer sopranos manufactured so that locating even one instrument in your locality might be impossible. There are also few used sopranos available, making it difficult to buy one. So, the first obstacle is to find and buy an instrument.

When one buys the instrument, one has to take care of both the price and quality. Many cheap instruments are advertised, many of them unable to play a true scale because of terrible intonation patterns. You get good sopranos from major manufacturers with an intermediate price, but whether you buy an intermediate instrument or a professional one, careful checking is vital to ensure the quality.

If you are not one who plays the saxophone at the highest professional level, you must get someone who is an expert to buy the instrument with you. This person could be a skilled colleague, a teacher, or a professional living near you. Find a music store that has two or more instruments for you to choose from. It is important to try many instruments of the same model to see which one is superior.

For those with prior experience in playing the saxophone, use your separate mouthpiece to test the instrument as using a new mouthpiece on a new instrument will create more confusion. Play only for a few minutes when you start on each instrument. You can cut short the choices by going with your instincts if you trust your first impressions. Check using a pitch tester (use a tuner), whether the key layout is comfortable (check the placement of pinky keys and palm keys) and check the extreme low and high register responses.

Breakpoint Check

This is an important initial item to address for a beginner learning the soprano saxophone. The breakpoint is the place where the mouthpiece and the reed come into contact. Against this fulcrum point, the reed vibrates. By doing this check, you will understand how much of the mouthpiece to place in the mouth. If you take little mouthpiece, the tone remains thin, pinched, and muffled. And if you take too much, the sound becomes loud, spread, and raucous.

Slip a piece of paper downward in the space between the mouthpiece table and reed to check for the breakpoint. Reposition this paper many times to come to its natural resting point and use a pencil to mark this point on the reed. Keep the left thumbnail on this mark and roll the thumb down until it rests flat on the ligature. When you bring the mouthpiece to begin practice, the thumb will hit your lower lip, and this will help you determine how much mouthpiece to take in.

Pitch Check

The second most significant item is the pitch check. Put the mouthpiece into your mouth after you have checked the breakpoint. Make use of your practiced embouchure, blow a well-supported above-average loud (mezzo forte) tone. This must have the sound of a concert C. When the embouchure is tight, it will sound higher. When the oral cavity setting and pressure are low, the pitch will sound flat. Make use of the best full tone using the mouthpiece alone. Many try to relax airstreams to get a lower pitch, but this technique is wrong. You can test the oral cavity setting and saxophone embouchure using this technique. So, keep the airstreams constant and fast. This mouthpiece check works on all kinds of saxophones with the pitches baritone (D), tenor (G), and alto (A).

SOPRANO SAXOPHONE EMBOUCHURE

We can describe this embouchure as having the properties of both an alto saxophone and clarinet setting. The jaw is a little down on the alto saxophone, and the corners push inwards. The muscles form a circle around the mouthpiece. We must raise the jaw and hold the corner muscles firm but pull back a little for the clarinet. In both cases, we need the raised jaw position. We need a more circular setting, as in the alto sax. We can describe the cavity position of the alto sax as Ah. For the soprano, we have a focused Eeu.

Problem Areas

The biggest problem area for the soprano saxophone is tone. It is easy to create a thin, bright, and weak tone with this instrument. If you use the checks mentioned earlier to set the oral cavity and establish the correct embouchure, it will help. Many classical players find #3 reed strength works best on tenor and alto saxophones while a#3h strength suits the soprano saxophone well. We assume the player uses the #3 Vandoren reed regular style so select the rest of the reed strengths in relation to this. The #3 V2 strength will become dark and warms up the soprano tone. It allows for excellent control because of the better embouchure setting.

INTONATION

For soprano saxophone players, the second biggest problem area is intonation. This is because the length of the tube is short compared to that of other saxophones. When you must change the pitch to a large extent, a little oral cavity or embouchure variation becomes necessary. Now you know the importance of making a careful check of the intonation pattern before buying. You will benefit if you have a trained soprano player with you to give you advice.

PALM KEY HEIGHT

Take careful note of the height of the palm keys. When the cork gets compressed on the key foot, the key will open too much, causing the upper notes to become sharp. It is normal to find Bb and B to be sharp in most cases. The solution to this problem is to use a four-by-two-inch piece of Dr. Scholl's Molefoam inside the saxophone bell. Place it directly on the other side of the low Bb and B tone holes. It will cause the bell diameter to decrease, and the acoustic effect is to lengthen the tube, lowering these tones.

HIGH CONSISTENCY OF THE NOTE

Another problem area is the high note consistency. Even though a saxophonist can play the instrument well, he will not master the upper two or three notes (high E, F#, and G). Players having expertise with the altissimo register on alto will find the secret lies in using the same oral cavity setting.

Approach the high E on the soprano through the F#/G as if they were altissimo G through Ab on the alto saxophone. It is not enough for the soprano player to use the palm keys but must rather change the oral cavity position to help the notes speak. When we need to articulate the notes, this area becomes more problematic.

You can use the syllable Hee to start an air attack pointed with the air stream alone. You can master this technique by practicing staccato eighth-note scales in the upper range.

One Suggested Practice Lesson

One may use the soprano to learn the repertoire of the Romantic, Classical, and Baroque periods. You can play the saxophone lightly to make it sound like a violin, oboe, or flute. When you play a piece written for this instrument, make sure you make it sound original, and it has all its characteristic dynamics. Make the dynamic range compact so that the forte is only delicate mf or strong mp. Players should make their transcriptions after buying original scores and then making the transcription of the solo part up a whole step. Writing the programs has become easy thanks to the computer. Players can also choose from many professional editions available. Listed below are some interesting pieces and exercises for the soprano saxophone.

1. The Rapid Staccato: Here is a way to make your tongue bounce on and off the reed at rocket speeds. Take a sharpened wooden pencil and bring it close to the eraser using your index finger and thumb. Keep your hand a few inches above a hard surface and drop the pencil's lead once on it. See how it continues to

bounce rapidly after you let it go. The loudest one is the first, and then the others are rebounds.

2. Except for the first instance, your fingers do not control the movement of the pencil. This is like the drummer hitting the snare drum at the beginning of a roll. Imitate this movement with your tongue for repeated notes:

   a) Play two rapid sixteenths open g.

   b) The first note is well-accented. And the second note is softer, reflecting the first. Think Ta La or Ta-Da.

   c) Now, play three notes TA -DA-DA or Ta la la.

   d) Follow this with the four-note sequence - Ta-da-da-da or Ta-la-la-la.

   e) Increase the number of notes to five, six, seven, and so on. Keep increasing the number of notes one at a time.

3. When the number of notes increases beyond five or six, counting becomes difficult. After you play open g, hold the instrument in your right hand and count the notes on the fingers of your left hand. Play up to 10 or 12 notes but accent only the first note. The following notes are effortless and softer, decreasing in intensity until it becomes nothing.

4. As you become familiar and confident with this exercise, you notice that the tongue movement has become automatic. It will shake, making a rapid staccato. You can use the air stream to copy the movement of a flag with your tongue. As you practice more, your tongue will bounce effortlessly at great speed.

5. Watch the ideal airflow speed and note the tongue's position and firmness when the rapid movement happens on its own.

6. Practice often with repeated notes from all registers. Try changing the dynamics, always accenting the first note and

making the other following notes softer. Once you get more fluency, try to change the notes instead of repeating them. This gives you the chance to play the various ascending and descending scales. After that, play across various registers and make sure the notes all sound even.

7. If the tongue's movements become stiff, make the rapid, repeated notes sound "th" as in the word the instead or la or da.

8. This will prove useful when the time comes for you to play challenging orchestral excerpts.

PRACTICE TECHNIQUES AND PHILOSOPHIES

We know well that each adult differs from each other. Everyone is special in subtle and obvious ways, large and small, that are physical or psychological. In the same way, our practice routines vary according to our likes and the demands of the times. It depends on our personalities and learning styles. We should never avoid the mechanical rigors of daily practice to strengthen the fundamentals of music. If a person has a short attention span and a distractible nature, he or she must put in the effort every day of the week, going over the same thing until there is room for doubt.

It doesn't matter whether the mouthpiece produces a sound that is neither dark nor bright, for it gives one the freedom to form the sound on the fly depending on what one is playing. The music might call for a lush and warm tone (such as Hodges) or dark and cool (like Desmond). The musician must maintain a flexible and solid home base embouchure that has a solid tonal center and consistent intonation. It is important to have a reliable teacher strong in the fundamentals to help with the regular exercises.

Sound and Tone Concepts

The cornerstone of tonal exercises is long tones, but the method of practice will vary each day. When you have a good focus, you can use a tuner and metronome to practice straight with no variety descending on the chromatic scale and ascending with good intonation in a smooth and even rate of decrescendo and crescendo. When one plays like this, it is easy to focus on other aspects of tone production, such as consistent and precise note attacks and releases.

Choose any hymn, set your metronome to a slow beat (such as the eighth note is 80), and play the song with an even tone. You can transpose different keys to work with different registers on the instrument. When you work like this, you can multitask when you work on the long tones and practice easy transpositions to help improve your skills as a saxophonist. The most useful transpositions are up a major sixth (from the concert score for alto players.). It is up a major second if you play soprano and up a perfect fifth if you read using a B-flat score. Hitting those transpositions each time keeps the mind and ears sharp.

Concepts Used During Practice

One way to practice involves playing a ballad from Peter Gabriel to Gershwin to Schubert and playing it many times, varying the song's emotion and color. You can learn a new tune and multitask, working on the tone. One must go through the lyrics to get a vibe and phrasing of the song. Think of color before you play the song - green, blue and imagine a feeling - a little wistful and try to evoke this while playing the melody.

When you play the song a second time, use different mood settings. Use dark red and deep sorrow, for instance. If you record yourself doing this practice, you will note the changes in the style of play. This helps you with the intonation and improves the inflection. This is an artistic advantage that you, as a saxophonist, have the freedom to shape to determine the character of the sound you play. There is a wide range of vocal expression in the woodwind instruments, so if you find a group of singers with different musical styles such as rock, pop, jazz, or opera, you learn how to change the intonation to carry the emotion from the others.

The harmonic or rhythmic content is secondary to the musician's ability to reach out to the audience using one's ability. Pick some singers like Sarah McLachlan, Frank Sinatra, Peter Gabriel, Joni Mitchell, or Billie Holiday and recreate their vocal colorings and phrasing styles with your intonation. Work with long tones and chorales to improve the quality of your saxophone tone. The character of your sound will distinguish you as an individual artist. Most of this tone will come from the rich history of the instrument with the capacity to produce a wide range of tones. The articulation is as important a component as the character and tonal quality. The most attractive saxophonists use articulation to punctuate and enhance the tone. If one wants to develop good jazz articulation, he must learn and play along with his favorite jazz compositions by ear alone. This helps him emulate the nuances and styles perfectly.

ARTICULATION AND STYLE

The top saxophone articulators are Sydney Bechet, Dick Oatts, Sonny Rollins, Joe Lovano, Wayne Shorter, and Charlie Parker. Play along with their songs and develop a flavor of their styles.

To develop the tongue technique, set the metronome at its slowest rate, a quarter note 40. Repeat the articulation syllable you wish to play - Ti, Di, Li, Tut, or Tu. Choose a single note from each instrument register and articulate a series of measures that you subdivide into increasing numbers.

For instance, start with two measures of two half notes. Then, use two measures of three half-note triplets and then four quarters followed by five-quarter quintuplets. Increase the number to six quarter note triplets and increase to 7 quarter septuplets, and so on, until you complete the full cycle. Or you can stop if you cannot tongue the subdivisions cleanly and evenly. Then move on to the next syllable. It is enough for you to use these two articulations. You must try to incorporate articulations in other regions of practice as well.

While practicing scales (suppose you are practicing harmonic major with a flatted-second) and their allied arpeggios, use a different syllable and tonguing pattern for each iteration. Suppose you play C major from prime to octave; try to use the Ti syllable for each note. Next, play the pattern from the supertonic to the ninth, use the di syllable with each upbeat. After you practice these for a few days and feel good, pep up the practice by, say, starting on the downbeat of one.

C-Ti followed by D-Di, E (without articulation), and then play F-Li. Again, G has no articulation, and the next note A is Tu. Play B without articulation and the last note C-Di. After this, mix and match the syllables in a more random way to emphasize unusual beats (such as downbeat of 2). You get used to the sound and tension of this beat soon.

OTHER PRACTICE ROUTINES

While playing classical etudes, apply these articulation games. You can also try them with improvisation exercises and transcribed solos. It is an interesting exercise, though performing them in public would need great courage or an enormous amount of practice. But one must keep practicing influencing every note that emerges from your instrument with your jazz sensibilities. When you are working or learning with a formal piece of classical music, spend an hour a day on the piece for a week until you get the hang of it, or you are so sick of it you cannot play it anymore. You can move to something else and come back at a later time to play this again.

SIGHT READING

Try sight-reading standard etudes from a variety of instruments and sight transpose them. Try the Two-Part Inventions text by Bach that he wrote for the piano. It has a great linear voice that leads to diatonic melodies that are easy to play and transpose to different keys. Another must-read is 48 Etudes by Ferling for Oboe or Saxophone and if you want to try something more difficult, try the 18 Exercises or Etudes by Berbiguier for Flute. It has melodic interval studies that are perfect for your saxophone. Whichever etude you plan to try, play it at an exceedingly slow rate at first.

TRANSCRIBING

Your aspirations as a jazz musician should lie towards transcribing improvised solos while practicing etudes. Transcribing is like the clean-and-jerk because it hones so many important aspects of playing. When you play by ear, it helps you achieve fluency in a few areas. You must write the piece you practice and analyze it as it helps you improve your style and vocabulary as a jazz improviser. You can begin with Charlie Parker because he is a talented musician and most of his solos are short and logical, while his vocabulary comprises the language of modern jazz. You should transcribe his solos, though not because it improves your vocabulary alone.

When you take a week off from regular practicing, think about the Charlie Parker solos, their phrasing, technique, and articulation. After you memorize the entire solo playing it note by note, think about how you will play it. Use different tempos to make phrase swings and change the keys. It is customary to choose the next key to use for transcribing the phrase or solo, such as by fourth or by a step. This helps you develop the confidence that you can play in any key, which may not be so if you were to learn by rote using a pattern to lock the fingers motor memory.

Philosophy

The only philosophy you should have is to play any tune in your head well. It is better to avoid memorizing licks and patterns and then regurgitate them. Instead, focus on being able to play the way your mind hears it. Improve the extent of your musical knowledge by listening to more music and concentrate on the interesting parts.

Practice

Though you may not sing melodiously, you can teach your fingers to play the melodies you want and sing beautiful tunes. Use the metronome and keep swinging your tunes and keys as much as you want. If possible, sing a tune first and then play it on the instrument. When you don't get it right, repeat the phrase. Listen to yourself play and make sure you are playing the way you want to. When you are successful, start the next phrase. Play it back to see whether you are doing it right. Once you can address yourself in this way, you can start playing using consequence from an antecedent manner.

This is a fun-filled exercise that will bring your fingers into the line of your mind and ears.

CHAPTER 10

SAXOPHONE ARTICULATION

Bring the tip of the tongue and touch the tip of the reed. About 1/32 inches from the tip, the flat underside of the reed must touch the top side of the tongue. You must use small up and down movements from the tongue to get the correct articulation. Instances of inaccurate articulation include:

a) Moving the tongue from the front to the back, in a circular movement, or sideways.
b) Moving jaw, lips, or throat.
c) Tonguing mouthpiece opening.
d) Tonguing with the underside or extreme tip of the tongue.
e) Anchor tonguing.
f) Tonguing roof of mouth or teeth.
g) Tonguing with air movement rather than the tongue.

It is important to correct any incorrect articulations as soon as they appear. If you develop a bad habit, it becomes difficult to correct it because you have to unlearn the bad habit first. The correct articulation syllable to use here is tah.

The tips of the reed and the tongue come in contact only for the slur's first note. You will not use the tongue movement for any of the other notes because you leave it in the stationary aaah position. When you make an incorrect articulation, your tongue will move while playing the notes under the slur. Use the correct articulation syllable taaaaa.

TYPES OF STACCATO

Two kinds of staccato are possible - air stop and tongue stop. In both cases, the articulation begins in the way described above. To do the tongue-stop staccato, one has to return the tongue to the reed end with the end of the note. This method is useful when playing fast repetitive passages. When performing the air-stop staccato, the player does not connect back to the reed to end the note. Instead, the diaphragm stops the flow of the air and ends the note. You must not use a cutting off movement of either the lower jaw or throat to stop the air.

This kind of play helps when the passage is semi-legato and slow. In such situations, an abrupt stop will not sound good. The correct articulation symbol is tah-[where a standard accent will have the variation as per the standard articulation. By following the articulation direction and adding a stronger tongue-stroke, we produce stress at the beginning of the note. If you have enough skill, you may add a slight push of the air to the beginning of the note. Here the correct articulation syllable will be Tah.

When you see a carrot or cap accent, it denotes a cross between staccato and an accent. To begin the accent, the tongue will strike the reed harder. You end the note with the tongue stop. The articulation syllable here is Taht.

It might be necessary to make the accent under the slur. For this, you can use one of the two methods given here:

1. Push a little from the diaphragm to stress the note.
2. When the passage is fast, the diaphragm will not affect it, and it will not make stress. Then you can articulate with the tongue.

The correct syllable for articulation is, huh.

We produce legato in the same way we articulate. The air must never stop between articulated notes, and we use the air in a constant flowing motion. Then, correct flowing legato will happen. The articulation syllable to use is tah.

Detached legato is a combination that uses a lengthened staccato. This kind of articulation makes a feeling of detached connection. You can produce this, but the best one is to use air-stopped staccato. Stretch the length of the notes until you get the desired note length. The correct articulation syllable is tah.

CHAPTER 11

MUSICAL MODES EXPLAINED

Here we investigate the concept of musical modes and their importance to making music. It is interesting but confusing for some because they all seem the same. The important questions to ask are:

- What is a mode?
- Do we use any special notes in modes?
- Why is there a flavor in modes?

Anyone who has searched around for knowledge in music will know all music is a type of mode. It is important to sift the information before you can start using modes creatively. There is a musical theory behind modes, and one has to study the examples, both harmonic and melodic, to understand how to use them in your compositions.

What is a Mode?

A mode is a kind of scale. They have alternate tonalities, but we can derive them from a major scale. This could be a traditional major scale that will use the Ionian mode. There are seven modes:

1. Ionian
2. Dorian
3. Phrygian
4. Lydian
5. Mixolydian
6. Aeolian
7. Locrian

Constructing the Mode

We construct the mode in different ways according to its structure.

    a) Adding a sharp to the major scale.

Ionian

This is the same as the major scale. So, if you are familiar with the major scale, you already know the Ionian mode.

Dorian

Starting from the major scale, we lower the third degree and seventh-degree one semitone.

Phrygian

In this, we lower the 2nd, 3rd, 6th, and 7th degrees one semitone.

Lydian

For making the Lydian, we raise the 4th degree one semitone.

Mixolydian

We have to lower the 7th degree one semitone.

Aeolian

You have to lower the 3rd, 6th, and 7th degrees one semitone.

Locrian

We lower the 2nd, 3rd, 5th, 6th, and 7th degrees one semitone.

    b) Change the tonic.

The tonic is the starting note of the major scale. The C major scale has the notes CDEFGABC. If you use the same notes but start from the second note D, we get the Dorian mode and we can derive all the modes in this way. If you start with the third note, you get the Phrygian, and if you begin with the fifth note, you get the Mixolydian. When you begin with the sixth note, the mode becomes Aeolian, and when you use the seventh note, the mode becomes Locrian.

The characteristic of this construction is that all the notes of the C major scale are present. By changing the mode, we place a different emphasis on the scale. One could use mnemonics to remember the different modes.

NOTES OF THE MAJOR SCALE

They are all notes of the major scale, but they differ in how the notes get emphasized. So, when we consider two modes, such as C Ionian and E Phrygian, all the notes remain the same, but the way we use them differs. In the Phrygian mode, the E note remains emphasized. The tone of the scale differs from that we get by using C as the root note. What we do is to establish the tonal center in the music.

ESTABLISH THE TONAL CENTER

In the melody, we may use different methods to establish the tonal center.

1. Repeat the tonic - By using a double note, we can change the scale's emphasis.
2. Change the place in the passage: When we begin the passage, we use the note first (or last) to give it prominence.
3. Emphasize dynamically: By increasing the velocity of the tonic, we can add accent to the note.
4. Change the range: In the range emphasis, we use a group of notes and include the tonic.
5. Emphasize using rhythm: We can place the note on downbeats or sustain the note longer to get the desired effect.
6. Use the Bassline: Use the note in the bassline or keep playing the tonic repeatedly.

All methods may not work well. You can see which one works when you practice and then adopt it. Keep the concept in mind and work towards establishing a tonal center.

THE ANGEL MODE AND DARK MODE

This part will seem unreal to some and mystical to others, but you will understand why some modes seem dark while others are light and happy when you play the modes. The simplest explanation is through the use of flats and sharp. When the mode has more flats, it seems dark, and when it has more sharps, it becomes happy. So, if you don't want your music to sound sinister, choose a mode that has more sharps.

Certain modes remain associated with specific emotions. For instance, the Ionian and Lydian modes help us play spiritually uplifting songs. We use Dorian and Mixolydian music to play gospel and blues music while, for playing sad songs, we make use of the Aeolian mode. When we need dramatic or scary music, we use Locrian and Phrygian music. To see whether you have a dark or light-scale, follow this chart:

Lydian: 1 2 3 #4 5 6 7 (Happiest)

Ionian: 1 2 3 4 5 6 7

Mixolydian: 1 2 3 4 5 6 b7 (Midrange happy)

Dorian: 1 2 b3 4 5 6 b7

Aeolian: 1 2 b3 4 5 b6 b7 (Midrange sad)

Phrygian: 1 b2 b3 4 5 b6 b7

Locrian: 1 b2 b3 4 b5 b6 b7 (Darkest)

We have a chord progression in the classic manner of the first, fourth, and fifth notes when we play major keys. If we choose the root C, these chord changes involve C, F major chord, and G major chord. We are so used to hearing this sound that it sounds right to us and there are thousands of songs that use these three chords.

Each mode has a set of extra chords that work well with it. These extra chords help make the tonal center and new melodies. You can also try using these chord progressions when writing new music.

Note: We use uppercase Roman numerals to represent major chords. To write minor chords, we use lowercase Roman numerals.

Ionian: I-IV-V7-I (C maj-F maj-G7-C maj)

Dorian: i7-ii-III-bVII-I 7 (C min7-D min-Eb maj-Bb maj-C min7)

Phrygian: i7-bvii7-v-bII-1 (C min7-Bb min7-G min7-Db maj-C min7)

Lydian: I-iii7-II7-vii7-1 (C maj-E min7-D7-B min7-C maj)

Mixolydian: I7-bVII7-IV-I7 (C7-Bb7-F maj-C7)

Aeolian: i7-bVII7-bVI-bVII7-i7 (C min7-Bb7-Ab maj-Bb7-C min)

We see how using the seven modes is a terrific way to explore new horizons and make new compositions. It is easy to program them using your sequencer. Better still, write it down on paper to work it out.

ANOTHER LOOK AT THE MODES

Let us have another look from another perspective.

We have seven modes in western music because each mode represents one unique starting note.

Ionian - C

Dorian - D

Phrygian - E

Lydian - F

Mixolydian - G

Aeolian - A

Locrian - B

We number them from 1 to 7, depending on the scale degree we use as the tonic. So, the Dorian begins on the second degree, and the next mode will have a tonic that increases in pitch. The Lydian mode of C major begins on the 4th degree, and this carries on until we reach the seventh degree.

Though it works that way, we will talk about their root note or tonic. We don't say we play this song in the Dorian mode based on the C major scale. Instead, we say that we play this song in D-Dorian, meaning the tonic is D.

CHANGE IN THE INTERVAL SEQUENCE

A significant thing happens when you move forward on the scale degrees. You are moving away from the major scale sequence by shifting the root. So, though we have a relatively easy construction, the sequence of intervals defines the typical scales through their key signatures. It doesn't matter which major scale you choose; the key signatures will determine the mode. Let us see what is happening from this perspective.

Interval of Notes Sequence

Ionian T T S T T T S

Dorian T S T T T S T

Phrygian S T T T S T T

Lydian T T T S T T S

Mixolydian T T S T T S T

Aeolian T S T T S T T

Locrian S T T S T T T

When we check the pattern, we see the symmetry when we arrange them according to their roots. Here, T represents tone or one whole note, while S represents the semitone or a half note. When you memorize the mode, you will get to know the features better. It is time to think about scale degrees and accents because you can apply them to all the minor and major scales.

You do not have to memorize any key signatures because the mode represents the scale. What you will need to understand is how the key signature changes. In this table, we will see how to work with the modes.

MODE INTERVAL SEQUENCE

Ionian 1 2 3 4 5 6 7

Dorian 1 2 b3 4 5 6 b7

Phrygian 1 b2 b3 4 5 b6 b7

Lydian 1 2 3 #4 5 6 7

Mixolydian 1 2 3 4 5 6 b7

Aeolian 1 2 b3 4 5 b6 b7

Locrian 1 b2 b3 4 b5 b6 b7

For those who have strong memories, learning this table will be easy. You will realize that the modes are the same scales with a different name.

- C Lydian
- D Mixolydian
- E Aeolian

- F# Locrian
- G Ionian
- A Dorian
- B Phrygian

Even though it looks silly, there is a great deal of significance to it whether you are working with chord charts or improvising a tune. The super jazz musicians will find it exciting to jump around the keys and experiment with modes.

CHARACTERISTICS OF THE MUSICAL MODE

We see each mode and its special features as a major or minor with a separate tone. This tone determines whether it belongs to jazz music or rock music.

IONIAN MODE

Degree of the mode: None

Interval of notes: TTSTTTS

Songs in this mode Beatles song - Let It Be

Ozzy Osbourne - Goodbye to Romance

As mentioned before, the Ionian mode is the major scale. Everybody loves the songs in this mode because of their lively and cheerful nature. All pop music uses this mode, and it is the easiest to work with because we don't have to vary the scale notes. The tension and releases come through the half-step between scale degrees 6 and 7. The 7th resolves back to the root, and the tension gets released using delineated loops in melody and integrated song segments. The song's innocent and happy style in the Ionian mode makes it the popular choice in the gospel, children's music, and pop music.

DORIAN MODE

Degree of the mode: 6

Interval of notes: TSTTTST

Songs in this mode Simon and Garfunkel - Scarborough Fair

America - A Horse with No Name

This mode has a minor triad in the lead, and so it feels like a minor scale. The 6th scale degree is natural and not flat, but the 7th is. Because of this, the mode has two peculiar properties. It sounds sad but not as much as the songs in the typical minor scale. And the 7th never resolves completely, so there is always a sense of restlessness. You can hear this in Irish and Celtic music, but those genres also have the influence of Bluegrass, Blues, Country, and Folk music. Songs you can hear in this group include Get Lucky (Daft Punk), Wicked Game (Chris Isaak), and Mad World (Tears for Fears).

PHRYGIAN MODE

Degree of the mode: b2

Interval of notes: STTTSTT

Songs in this mode Stu Phillips - Knight Rider Theme

Jefferson Airplane - White Rabbit

In this mode, we experience an ambiguity of sound so that the reader is unsure of what he hears. The 2nd degree is flat, which confuses most people who expect to hear a whole step at this point for both minor and major scales in Ionian mode.

People do not use this much in film scores because of this. You can create a sense of tension, dread, and mystery or show an impending terrible event but keep the warmth in the music. Typically, metal and classical bands use this. We also call it the Spanish Gypsy Scale.

LYDIAN MODE

Degree of the mode: #4

Interval of notes: TTTSTTS

Songs in this mode: Danny Elfman - The Simpsons Theme

Hoyt Curtin - The Jetson's Theme

This mode bears resemblance to the Ionian in that the first chord is a major triad. What is surprising and unexpected are the intervals. The difference lies in the fourth degree that remains raised one semitone. Otherwise, they have the same Ionian tone of happiness and cheerfulness.

It is natural for the fourth to want to resolve into the 5th. Musicians use this to their advantage while making their music. Many show tunes and the jazz genres exploit this to engage their audiences.

MIXOLYDIAN MODE

Degree of the mode: b7

Interval of notes: TTSTTST

Songs in this mode: Beatles - Norwegian Wood

Lynyrd Skynyrd - Sweet Home Alabama

We can change one note in the Ionian to get the Mixolydian mode. We flatten the 7th degree to do this. The Mixolydian mode is a wonderful choice for solo improvisations in a major key because of an unfamiliar counterpoint that makes everything exciting.

We hear this music scale in lots of country and rock songs on the major scale. It provides a smooth and less than significant sound in an otherwise merry song. There is the same sense of not resolving like the Dorian, which the musician can exploit.

AEOLIAN MODE

Degree of the mode: b6

Interval of notes: TSTTSTT

Songs in this mode: REM - Losing My Religion

Katy Perry - I Kissed a Girl

This mode gives us the natural minor scale. In this, we get the modern blues sound that combines resentment, sadness, despair, and regret. We find many songs in the rock music genre use this sound because it combines well with the minor pentatonic scale. There is a sense of a fallback to the 50s at times because it has flattened 6 and 7 scale degrees instead of natural. There are thousands of songs in this mode because it is the minor key. Bob Dylan's All Along the Watchtower and Walking on the Moon by The Police are well-known examples.

LOCRIAN MODE

Degree of the mode: b5

Interval of notes: STTSTTT

Songs in this mode: Metallica - Ride the Lightning

Bjork - Army of Me

The special feature of the Locrian mode is its flat fifth degree. This gives it the characteristic darkness and, because of this diminished fifth chord, you see little use of this mode in western music that depends so much on the major I and V chords. This has led many composers to say that this mode is purely theoretical, with no practical use in actual music.

The sound is very dark, evoking a sense of sadness combined with brooding anger. On occasions, you will hear it in metal songs and classical compositions. It expresses darkness and dissent more than the other modes.

Getting to learn how the modes operate and the way to construct them helps you get into the groove of your favorite genre. It makes your songs more expressive and truer to emotions.

CHAPTER 12

CREATE PRACTICE METHODS AND STAY INSPIRED

Squeaking is natural but unexpected for the beginner. The way around it is to practice for around two hours every day until your sax obeys you completely. The squeaks or chirps occur when a note sounds a harmonic (or overtone), and you didn't mean it to.

GET COMFORTABLE BEFORE YOU BEGIN

Sounds great, but what is it? This means you have a good place to practice (meaning you are not disturbing anyone), your instrument is in excellent condition, and there is no distraction. Be sure that you do not have any commitments for an hour at least. Assemble the sax and sit comfortably to begin practice.

SET-UP PRACTICE SPACE

For the serious student of music, practice space is essential. It shows he has the determination and a schedule for his practice. If your house is small, you must find another place like a music room or playground.

Get a Room

If there is a playroom where there are no people, this is ideal for your sax practice. If you cannot do this, make a separate soundproof booth for one. But this is a pricey option, so think about other choices before you consider this.

If you can shut yourself in your soundproof room, it will be the best option. Close the doors and windows and play the sax. Ask your brother or sister to stay outside and check whether they can hear the sax. If they cannot, then your room is soundproof. There will be at least one room in the house that is soundproof, so be sure to check all the rooms.

Practice on a Bridge

No, seriously, the best place is on a bridge or any secluded public place where you do not have too many people. The bridge remains deserted, usually because people are moving from one end to the other, but no one lingers. If you go practice your sax there, you will disturb no one. One of the most famous sax players, Sonny Rollins, used to practice on a bridge for three hours every day.

Use the Open Air

The other practical option is to go to a huge open field for your sax practice.

Practice in Your Car

If you have an RV, a truck with a camper shell, or a van, you can practice there. Make sure there is no sound coming out when you close the vehicle. Also, make sure there is enough legroom, or you will soon get cramped. For those with a large vehicle, you can park in a quiet spot and start playing. You can use some recordings from the stereo system of your vehicle and play along. Or roll down the windows and conduct a one-man show in town in your car.

USE A SAXOPHONE MUTE

There is a company that makes saxophone mutes. You get a casing that covers your sax and has holes through which you put your hands in and start playing. You also get a saxophone jack so you can hear what you are playing. Using the audio jack, you can make recordings of your practice sessions. It is a great option for those who cannot practice in their apartments because of their neighbors and don't have any open space nearby.

CHECK YOUR INSTRUMENT

The saxophone is a complex instrument with so many parts. You need to make sure everything works to get the best out of your practice session.

Use a Magnificent Mouthpiece

First, get a mouthpiece that reflects your dedication. A cheap mouthpiece will make the sound bad. Even when your sax is a low-cost instrument, using a terrific mouthpiece will make it sound wonderful. The same thing holds for reeds. Do not save money when you buy your reed. Buy one from an established manufacturer like Vandoren or Rico Royal.

Buy a Sax Stand

This is the best way to get inspired. Buy a sax stand and put it there in front where you can see it all the time. You are always ready to pick it up and play, and this is the best motivation for any beginner.

Wear a Comfortable Sling

The sling is the piece of strap you wear around the neck. Wearing this makes saxophone playing comfortably. The one that comes with your sax will be a cheap one that will soon cut into your shoulders. Check on eBay for a comfortable foam sling for $20 or $30. Be sure to buy one that has squishy, fat foam around it so it will add to your comfort.

Avoid Distractions

Do not practice where there is a lot of noise or people constantly moving around. Try to choose a secluded nook where there is enough protection from the light and wind. If your brother and sister are likely to disturb you, make sure they don't. Tell them you are practicing and lock your room.

Start with Your Scales

If you are not sure where to begin, start with the scales. If possible, play the scales over a backing track. You get accuracy and develop a magnificent sound when you use a track backing the scale you play. Then try to practice without the backing track. See how it sounds and then choose the better option. Adding the track to the key you are playing adds relevance to your practice and it will encourage you to play for a long while and allow you to develop more confidence.

Ask Permission

If you are going to make a noise, it is better to get permission as your practice might disturb your neighbors. When this is the case, it is better to get permission than to go around apologizing when the complaints pour in. It is a simple thing to do and if there are people who object, make sure you practice when they are not around.

Practice Breathing

To play the saxophone, you need more breath than other instruments. Make the flow of the breath constant to develop a stable sound and to control the flow of air, train your throat and diaphragm. This comes only through practice, so play the instrument at least for 15 minutes on a tight-schedule day and for one hour on others.

Make sure you use your diaphragm for breathing. Your lungs expand downwards - imagine that someone is going to hit you in the stomach. Push the abdomen out as this is the best way to breathe properly.

Practice Often

To develop your embouchure, practice often. When it is easy to get your sax out, it becomes easy to practice. So, make sure it is accessible always.

Transcribe a Solo

If you wish to develop into a talented saxophonist, you must learn to transcribe solos by prominent saxophone artists. What is the meaning of transcribing? To transcribe, one must listen to the solos they wish to learn, write the notes they hear, and play it exactly as the other artist plays it. You could also play along, meaning you could play the track and play the sax along with it. But you will not develop much accuracy, and the speed of learning will be slow.

Transpose Your Favorite Song

If you wonder how to transpose a song, it is simple. What we do is move (trans) the position (pose) of the notes of the song. We change the key of the song to a more convenient one.

When the song is in a key that makes it difficult for you to reach the high notes, you move the key down to sing all the notes comfortably. Do this for as many songs as you can so that you become confident of playing all the songs you want on your saxophone.

At the end of the day, it is satisfying to play a scale with no false notes. And you can play a low pianissimo if you have no leaks.

CHAPTER 13

SAXOPHONE MAINTENANCE TIPS

1. Go over the pads and check for seating and splits, including the octave keypads. If any need replacing, change them.
2. Check the working of the octave key. Play G and use the octave key - the pad must remain closed on the neck vent. The pad on the body vent must open and close. Now, finger A and operate the octave key. The pad on the neck vent must open and close, while that on the body vent must remain closed. Lubricate as necessary. If it does not work properly, call a repairman.
3. Play the middle finger C. The little pad above the first finger of the left hand must close. If you have a Yamaha saxophone, change to the left stack screw. On others, use the services of a repairman to shim with felt or cork.
4. Finger from 1 to 4 and from 1 to 5 Bb. See if the change is proper by depressing the B key. Above the F pad, you will have the set screw that you can adjust.
5. Now finger D while working the G# key. The tone should not change, and the G# pad must remain closed. In the event it opens even a little, the low B, Bb, and C# will remain prevented from

speaking. This prevents the proper use of the G# fingering articulations. Change the G# setscrew.

6. Advanced players can check the low intonation of B, C, C#, D, and Eb. Adjust felt bumpers using a good tuner.

7. Use pad dopes to soften the pads even when they are new. It will extend the life of the pads. You will benefit by paying for the swab and pad dope.

8. Use cork grease to lubricate the neck cork. You can use Vaseline or Chapstick while sewing machine oil remains a popular choice for many. You must oil the keys about every six months.

9. Wipe the saxophone with a damp cloth and buff dry. Use Pledge to wax two to three times a year. Another alternative is to spray Runyon Lacquer Life. If you have a student line sax with keys of silver color, there is no need for special attention because they are nickel-plated. You only need to wipe dry.

10. Remove the ligature and reed from the mouthpiece when you store the instrument. Use lukewarm water to wash the mouthpiece and wipe it dry with a soft cloth or tissue. Make use of a baby bottle nipple brush if needed. If there are saliva stains, soak the mouthpiece overnight in vinegar. Always have 6-8 reeds with you.

11. Use a good reed guard holder such as Lavos Reedguard VI or Vito to keep the reeds. Never leave it in the plastic container it comes in. Avoid playing the same reed for over two days. When you play the reeds using a rotation schedule, they will last much longer.

12. Keep the neck and mouthpiece wrapped in soft cloth such as socks, or commercial bags meant for the mouthpiece and neck. Do not let them rattle around in the accessory compartment. Mouthpieces get damaged beyond repair when you leave them like this.

13. Use bubble wrap around the instrument when you transport the instrument by vehicle. If you use a gig bag, make sure you carry the

instrument in your hand at all times and hold it in your lap during the trip. You can use compact cases that come with the strength and rigidity to give your instrument the needed protection.

14. Pro Pac Contoured Cases (Pro-Tech), Winter Flight Cases, and gig cases by Selmer Walt Johnson are the best.

CLEAN THE BODY OF THE SAXOPHONE

Use the Swab (Pull Through)

The swab is a cloth with a piece of string attached and a slight weight attached at the end. You can either buy this or make it by attaching a weight to a piece of any string strong enough to pull the swab and the weight. Attach a chamois or soft cloth to the string. The string must be longer than the length of the saxophone, so check this first. Your weight must be smaller than the top opening. Likewise, the cloth must also fit snugly in the opening but large enough to touch the instrument's sides as it flares out.

When it is time to clean the sax, pop the weight into the bell and turn the horn upside down. The weight will come out of the opening where the neck goes. You can pull the pull through and it is easy to clean the inside using a soft cloth. Do not use cleaning product or polish because if it gets on to the pads, it might them and shorten their life.

Tips

a) For the weight for the sash, use any piece of metal such as lead. It is preferable to cover it with plastic or leather so that it does not scuff the insides of the saxophone.

b) You will have to pull the pull-through twice to make the saxophone clean. Be sure to pull slowly to give the insides a thorough rub.

c) Commercial pull-throughs have a chimney sweep kind of bristle behind the cloth. This holds the cloth firmly to the sides and cleans well.

The Pad Saver

This resembles a fluffy branch and will go inside the body. It helps collect water from the wide parts of the bore. But because they don't reach the bottom, they are not good for clearing the whole instrument. One must not leave this inside the saxophone without giving your instrument a chance to dry out completely first. Clean it often with some warm water and detergent, after which you must rinse it and dry it out well.

Choose the Pad Saver or the Swab?

Each has its pros and cons, so it is better to go with both. Be aware that many dealers will sell you products to prevent the pads from sticking. These products do not serve any purpose. It might work for a day or two, but any kind of liquid or powder will attract dirt. So, instead of solving it, the problem will become bigger.

Cleaning might not solve all your problems. A loose, bent, or weak spring might cause problems. If you are not familiar with the mechanism, visit your repair shop or use a tool to re-tension the spring. It might be enough to use the tip of a pencil or a screwdriver. If the problem happens due to the build-up of goo, use lighter fluid with a pipe cleaner. Close the pad and place a clean rag with lighter fluid on it and gently pull it through. If you are in a hurry, you can use a clean piece of paper (in a cinch, a dollar note will do).

PAD CLAMPS

This also serves no useful purpose. If your pads have their proper seating, then there is no need for the clamps. If not, then in the short term, the clamps will help. Either way, a trip to the repairer is best. It is also likely that the clamps might damage the sax because they compress the normally open pads more than one held close by a spring. This makes the felt and leather lose some of their springiness.

CLEAN THE MOUTHPIECE AND INSIDE OF THE NECK

Though you can find the pad saver or swab to do this work, using a bottle brush helps more. You can also use a toothbrush to clean with detergent and then rinse it with tap water. People use antiseptic mouthwash as it helps. Clean it once a week or more. If you do not, you will find very nasty gunk building up inside the saxophone.

You will then have to take it to your repairer to get it cleaned. You can also use fluffy brushes, but make sure you don't leave them inside the saxophone when you pack it away.

If you find the build-up is bad, soak the region with detergent and water. You can also try to loosen the gunk by adding some vinegar first.

CLEAN THE OUTSIDE OF THE SAXOPHONE

It is better to use plain cloth for this. If you buy the cleaning cloth commercially, it will save you a great bit of trouble because commercial cleaning cloths have in-built cleaning qualities, so you will not need any polish. Remember polish can get on to your springs and pads or inside the rods, and this will cause more problems.

CHAPTER 14

MYTHS ABOUT THE SAXOPHONE

Many people stop playing the saxophone because they heard something adverse about it. There will be news about everything, including the saxophone, but one has to exercise caution on what is true and what isn't. It is not always easy to tell the truth from rumor or fake news and there is much of both about the saxophone. Here, we will discuss the most common ones so that you are clear about what to believe and which to discard.

Myth #1 You Must Practice 24-Hours a Day to Master the Sax

Yes, this is true. You cannot become a master without putting in hours of practice. It is true you can put in a few minutes each day and become an expert, but it depends on what kind of practice you do. It depends on the process and not on the amount of time, so it is better to aim for a better process than for the timeline.

Many students use an acknowledged practice - proper hold, proper posture, and the right exercises such as scales and arpeggios meant for beginners.

Myth #2 The Size of Your Oral Cavity Makes a Difference to the Sound

A lot of research has gone into this aspect of saxophone playing. They used simulated systems to check which aspects - oral cavity and lips, windpipe, and an artificial embouchure - impact the ease and fluency of play. Even a slight change in pressure on the embouchure causes a big change in the sound quality. There was no change when the volume and surface of the simulated oral cavity changed. When you change the volume of the oral cavity in your mouth, there is a change in the embouchure, creating the change. So, this myth is not true.

Myth #3 If You Play Fast Improvised Lines it Makes You Sound Good

Though this is a misunderstood concept, many people think this is true. Great improvisations have fast-moving passages with lots of changing notes, making the passage sound wonderful. One must try to establish a strong rhythm by controlling the airflow instead of getting more notes. The student must try to get a melody in the music and execute passages with musical and rhythmic value. Playing fast is not going to prove anything if it doesn't sound good. One must not aim for unrealistic values but rather play at their level of expertise. Even when you can play fast, it is better to play smoothly and fluently rather than fast. This myth is false.

Myth #4 Some Types of Saxophones are More Suitable for Jazz

It is the truth that the saxophone player contributes to 90% of the sound that the instrument makes. The mouthpiece colors this sound and adds flavor to the sound. One can also adjust the reed setup to get further refinement in the sound. The instrument directs the sound to the note, and that is that. The choice of instrument will add to the sound quality, but it is hard to say which color or flavor of sound remains the best for jazz or any other genre. So, this myth is false.

Myth #5 Practice Overtones and Get Into the Altissimo Range

This is true and not a myth. Practice playing overtones if you want to exploit the full range of the instrument. The myth in this connection is they say you need a high-baffle mouthpiece to play the overtone but there is nothing wrong with playing with a low-baffle mouthpiece to get reliable altissimo notes. Even when you play with high baffle mouthpieces, it is not true that the altissimo notes are easy to play. So, this myth is not true. And you must practice and perfect overtones if you want to progress as a saxophone player.

Myth #6 The Body of the Sax Must Be Resonating

It does seem to make sense that a resonant body will produce more resonant sound, but this is absurd. The saxophone's sound comes from the vibrating air column and not from the body or the finish. So, this is a myth. Instruments made with expensive material will sound better, but it is because of the superior design and construction and not because of the material alone. In the saxophone, the walls contain the air column but do not contribute significantly to the resonance or vibration.

Myth #7 Vintage Horns Give You a Vintage Sound

Remember, the sound comes from the person playing the instrument and not from its style or age. When you play the saxophone, you must have a proper approach, the proper posture, and a wonderful technique to produce a terrific sound. To get the right sound, one must avoid mistakes and do the right thing to get the proper sound. You will get a great sound even when you use a cheap instrument, so this myth is not true.

Myth #8 Ligatures Will Improve or Destroy the Sound

Here we have another myth. Ligatures make a difference because when you use the ligature, the saxophone will sound better but the role of the ligature is to hold the reed in place and nothing more. It is not there to influence the sound in any way. When the ligature breaks, have improper securing, or improper placement, the sound's quality will decrease and you will not get the full, vibrant sound you expect from your saxophone.

Myth #9 You Must Perfect a Concept Before You Can Move On

Many students will start something before they have finished what they are working on. Though this might have its uses, in the general sense, it will slow your progress. New students find they have mastered the subject with one glance at it and they want to proceed to the next topic, but this is not a good idea. Have a second opinion from your teacher before you try to move to the next subject. Revisit the old topic many times over an extended period, so you develop your understanding and fluency. After you finish the course, go back to the beginning and start again. It is not easy to understand a musical concept the moment you have seen it. So, though you must perfect the technique before moving on, it is better to avoid getting bogged down in one topic for a long time.

Myth #10 The Best Saxophone is the Selmer MKVI

Professionals always wanted the Selmer MKVI because it had terrific ergonomics. Many say it was only aggressive marketing, and there was nothing spectacular about it. MKVIs can create wonderful sounds, but the sound quality is subjective, with many players opting for other brands. The reason for their huge cost is people have associated the MKVIs with the golden era of jazz from the mid-50s to the 60s. So, even though many instruments surpass the MKVI in intonation, ergonomics, and sound, they remain a symbolic inspiration for new users who want to play jazz music.

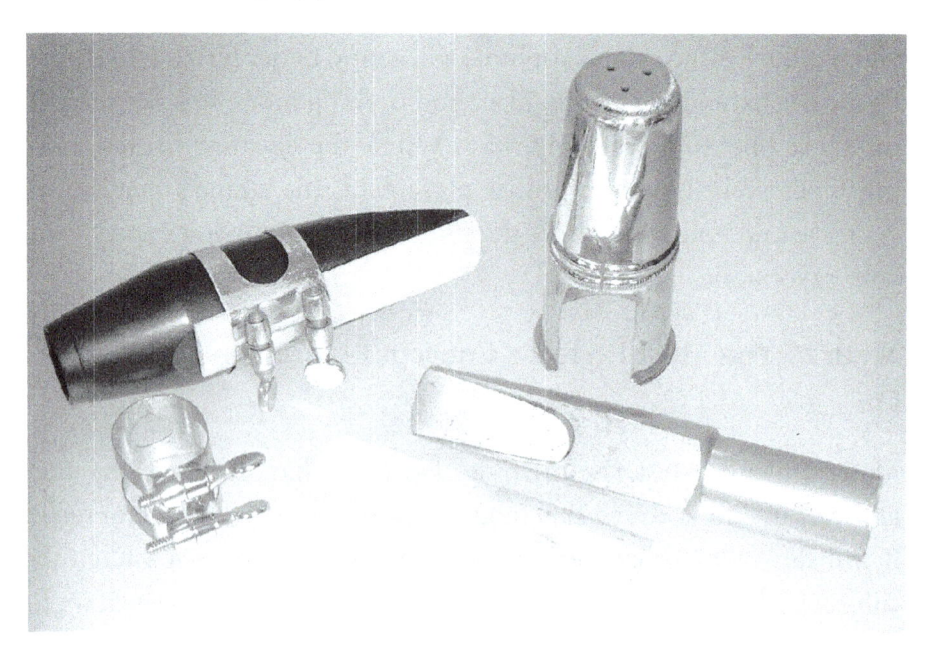

Myth #11 Metal Mouthpieces Have a Brighter Sound Than Those of Hard Rubber

This is not true. The mouthpieces' material does affect things like comfort and smoothness of grip, but it will not change the way the saxophone sounds. The shiny appearance of the metal mouthpiece will tempt you to say that the sound is brighter, but it is not so. The factors affecting sound are the height of the baffle, the width of the chamber, and the use of a proper embouchure.

Myth #12 When Two Teachers Tell Two Different Things, One of Them Must be Wrong

Students will often come across two conflicting statements when they have more than one teacher in the class. You needn't worry about this because both pieces of information may be true. By watching YouTube videos, you can get plenty of information on embouchures, altissimo fingerings, what to practice, and articulation. Often, there is more than one contradiction to this information. If you face such a situation, listen to the teacher you like and whose style of playing is agreeable with you. It is difficult to grasp things immediately by looking at one perspective alone. If you get any suggestions, always give them a try before you move on to another thing. There is a chance that one of them is saying something wrong but being teachers, they must have a grasp on the subject, and so it pays to listen.

Myth #13 Only if You Have a Fancy Ligature Will You Sound Good

Having a fancy, expensive ligature will make your sax look good but it does not change the way your sax sounds. The only thing one expects from the ligature is that it holds the reed in place and allows free vibration. All the cheap ligatures will do all this without any change or any application of skill. Do not worry about the influence of the ligature because it doesn't matter at all. Fit one over your mouthpiece and start playing the instrument.

Myth #14 You Get What You Pay For

This is true and there is another step to this - get the best mouthpiece you can get. When you pay more, you get better quality. This is true of all things in life, and it is true for the saxophone also. There isn't any magic "quality" that you can get without paying for it. Some manufacturers spend a lot of effort and use high-quality materials to make the best saxophone. If you want to get the best saxophone, you need to spend money. Be careful about spending your money on fake items because you will likely end up with poor quality items.

Myth #15 You Have Learn a Lot of Scales and Theory Before Being Able to Improvise

This myth is not true. You can improvise with a single note. All you need to do is to use your imagination. Improvising brings great joy, so you get inspired to do more when you improvise for the first time. This is possible in the lowest level, where you know what the next note is. But when you want to play complex passages, you will need more knowledge, such as that of scales. When you know the pattern of the scales, you can improvise at that level.

Myth #16 The Best MKVIs are Those Made from WWII Cartridge Shells

This myth probably came into existence in France, where plenty of cartridge shells were lying around. But there is no truth in the statement that the WWII cartridge shells make the best MKVIs. But there is one thing – the cartridge shells were made out of one specific material known as cartridge brass, but Selmer never made MKVIs from recycled cartridge shells.

Myth #17 You Should Learn the Saxophone When You are Young

You can become a magnificent saxophone player if you begin to play when you are young. But no rule says you cannot learn the sax when you are older. Learning the sax requires effort and dedication. When you are young, this is easy while older people find concentrating and making an effort difficult. So, it is true that one must learn the saxophone when one is young.

Myth #18 As You Progress on the Saxophone, You Should Use Harder Reeds

Beginners tend to use soft reeds. When we use soft reeds, the pressure needed to make a stable tone will be less and this will help beginners during the first few weeks. You will migrate to harder reeds soon, and it will be easy to make altissimo range and high notes. But lower notes will not be easy to make, and the dynamics are sluggish. The softer reeds help you get a more versatile sound. To get the high notes, you will have to work on the air column control.

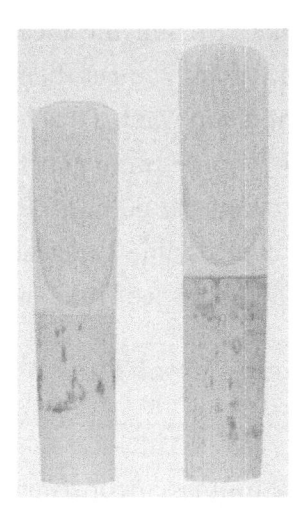

Myth #19 China Makes Terrible Horns

Some time back, all the horns the Chinese made were terrible. They had issues with the intonation and made lots of strange noises. The metal alloy's quality was horrible, and the soldering used to come off within a short time. They couldn't stay in tune, and they were lousy.

But these days, the Chinese models are up to the mark. And the quality is improving all the time. But it pays to be careful with the instrument you buy.

Myth #20 You Must Play the Same Sax Your Teacher Plays

This is one of the oldest myths around. If you play the same instrument as your teacher, you will follow his instructions with ease. One can follow the movements of the teacher and learn fast but what is good for one is not so for the next. Student saxophones are easier to play, though the sound will not be so good.

Myth #21 If You Practice Fast, You Can Play Fast

This is a myth many beginners fall for. You indeed need to practice fast tempos to be able to play fast. But the idea of playing is to get the rhythm and tempo right. When you get them right, you will have the ability to play at any tempo you want. To achieve this, you can start at a slower pace first. Say that you want to play the 16th note at 120 bpm. You must start by practicing it at 60 bpm. Practice it until you get it smooth rhythmically. Then, double the speed to 120 bpm. Use the metronome at the same 60 bpm speed but play twice as fast.

Myth #22 You're Playing Out of Tune Because of Your Instrument

Every saxophone has tuning inconsistencies. Some are more inconsistent than the others but, in the end, it is the player who plays in tune and not the instrument. We must learn to listen and match the pitch of the group and sing along. The saxophone cannot do it alone without you.

Myth #23 You Must Re-Pad Your Sax Every Five Years

Only poor-quality saxophones need repadding and overhauling. We replace them because they are of poor quality in the first place. Also, they were not set well and so they will leak within a short time. It might also happen when you don't swab out the horn after each practice session to remove the excess moisture.

When you have high-quality, well-installed pads, you can be sure they will last for a long time.

Myth #24 Lacquer Will Influence the Sound

This myth is not true. The finish or lacquer on the saxophone does not affect the sound of the saxophone. All brass instruments need some kind of protection and the lacquer finish is present for aesthetic purposes alone.

CONCLUSION

Having gone through the entire book, you will have a good idea about what to do and where to start with your saxophone playing. The aim of this book, "Saxophone for Beginners," is to get you into the groove and set you off on your musical journey.

I hope you enjoyed going through the book. It is now up to you to set sail across the musical ocean and discover where your talents lie. It might be in playing solos, or it could be with a band.

Whichever it is, the sooner you begin, the faster you will know. Here is wishing you the best on your magical voyage. Good Luck!

REFERENCES

CMUSE https://www.cmuse.org/CMUSE (2020, February 13). CMUSE. https://www.cmuse.org/best-beginner-saxophone-student/

Harry. (2021, January 08). Top 8 Best Tenor Saxophone Reviews [year]: Cheap and Pro Saxes. https://windplays.com/best-tenor-saxophones/

How to Play the Saxophone Saxophone fingering. (n.d.). https://www.yamaha.com/en/musical_instrument_guide/saxophone/play/play002.html

Pete, 8, K., Kim, 21, P., Author, P., 16, A., . . . 30, P. (2020, April 14). Fake news - 10 saxophone myths I Taming The Saxophone. https://tamingthesaxophone.com/myths-fake-news

Staff, C. (2021, January 12). Top 3 Best Soprano Saxophones [year]: Reviews. https://consordini.com/best-soprano-saxophone/

The Structure of the Saxophone Learn the names of the parts. (n.d.). https://www.yamaha.com/en/musical_instrument_guide/saxophone/mechanism/